Transforming Justice, Transforming Lives

Transforming Justice, Transforming Lives

Women's Pathways to Desistance from Crime

April Bernard

LEXINGTON BOOKS
Lanham • Boulder • New York • London

Published by Lexington Books
An imprint of The Rowman & Littlefield Publishing Group, Inc.
4501 Forbes Boulevard, Suite 200, Lanham, Maryland 20706
www.rowman.com

Unit A, Whitacre Mews, 26-34 Stannary Street, London SE11 4AB

British Library Cataloguing in Publication Information Available

Library of Congress Control Number: 2015950326
ISBN: 978-1-4985-1980-9 (cloth : alk. paper)
eISBN: 978-1-4985-1981-6

∞™ The paper used in this publication meets the minimum requirements of American National Standard for Information Sciences—Permanence of Paper for Printed Library Materials, ANSI/NISO Z39.48-1992.

Printed in the United States of America

Contents

Foreword

The Virtues of Interruption

The former US Secretary of State Madeleine Albright has been quoted as saying "Women have to be active listeners and *interrupters*—but when you *interrupt*, you have to know what you are talking about." This is a book about a group of women who are interrupters. Literally, the subjects of this research are sometimes described as "violence interrupters" following the Alex Kotlowitz documentary titled *The Interrupters* chronicling one of the most innovative crime reduction projects in the United States. Yet, the book is also about the idea of female interruption in a broader, more interesting way.

Interruption is a funny concept, certainly an unusual concept to organize such an important effort around. Whereas a "ceasefire" or a "cure" implies a dramatic break—the kind of forceful reversal promised by every magic bullet effort of crime prevention—an "interruption" is something rather different. According to most definitions, an interruption is a temporary break in some continuity, often a break in some external narrative with the interjection of a challenging or contrasting view. An interruption is not necessarily about shutting something down permanently, but about breaking the flow, forcing a reconsideration of direction.

Interruptions can be hugely annoying—cell phones ringing in the middle of a funeral eulogy, for instance. Indeed, no less a figure than John Locke wrote "there cannot be greater rudeness than to interrupt another in the current of his discourse," and it is hard to argue with that. On the other hand, sometimes the current of discourse around certain issues is such that a bit of interruption is absolutely necessary. Sometimes silent acquiescence in the face of self-defeating and false prophecy is the real danger, and what is needed is someone who can stand up and suggest another way.

The interrupters in this book are interrupting the flow of a number of taken-for-granted societal narratives. First, they have torn up the pages of the script that was written for them as gang-involved, stigmatized, drug-using women. Each knows precisely the role that society expects of them as victims turned perpetrators—they are the truly disadvantaged, the no-hopers, the nameless statistic who winds up dead in an alleyway somewhere anonymous. Yet, each has rejected that fate and rewritten an identity in a way that epitomizes the process of redemption.

Their primary means of doing so, of course, is also through "othermothering" in their communities, interrupting the cycle of shame, disrespect and retaliation—the endless loop of eye for an eye for an eye for an eye that of course leaves whole communities blinded in the wake of violent retribution. There is little surprise that women, like the incredible subjects of this book, are taking a vital leadership role in this growing peacemaking movement. In the end, if there was to be an interruption in the violence of poverty, deprivation and retaliation, it was always going to need women to be involved in the interrupting. How are men alone going to interrupt violence when violence is such a male noise to begin with? We already know how men interrupt violence, we dive in with more violence—from George Zimmerman's neighborhood "watch" to Ryker's Island's brutal efforts at juvenile "correction." Our interruptions only seem to make the noise louder.

The bigger surprise is that these innovative efforts emerge out of a process of personal redemption for individuals, and are therefore inseparable from the process of desistance from crime as described in this book, mixing the personal with the political, or the micro- with the meso- and the macro- as detailed in the author April Bernard's insightful analysis.

Finally, the women's stories in this book are also interrupting another long-standing and equally dangerous American myth that equates the beautiful concept of justice with punitiveness. Bernard weaves their incredible stories into an alternative vision of justice based on the notions of human interdependence, mutual stewardship, universal social concern, and most of all, Ubuntu. This transformative vision questions our taken-for-granted assumptions of how justice should work and what a justice system is for in ways that will appeal to many contemporary readers. After all, Bernard writes that, "Now perhaps more than any time in the recent history of the United States of America, there appears to be a widening of the window of opportunity for changing the discourse on crime and justice away from the deterrence-oriented and State-centered options that led to the war on crime and toward increasingly humanist alternatives." If she is right about this, and I sincerely hope she is, then this is precisely the right book for precisely the right moment.

Indeed, as wise and insightful as all of the interviewees quoted in this book truly are, the most remarkable interrupter in the book may be the author herself. April Bernard is a new voice in criminology in more ways than one.

Hers is not a household name (yet) in mainstream criminology, but more importantly the ideas and perspectives she brings to this book are themselves new, certainly outside of the stale predictability of the major US criminology departments and criminal justice agencies. This is something new, something a bit startling, even jarring—a break from the usual academic churning. Like with the best interruptions, I hope the rest of us will stop, if just for a moment, listen, think, and question just where we are heading.

Shadd Maruna, Dean
Rutgers University
Newark School of Criminal Justice

Acknowledgments

This book is inspired by the work of Ameena Matthews whose fearless dedication as a female violence interrupter was depicted in the documentary *The Interrupters* (2011), co-produced by Steve James and the acclaimed author Alex Kotlowitz. The film captures the nature and spread of violence in Chicago and the innovative interventions by violence interrupters working for CeaseFire Illinois to prevent retaliation and resolve conflict in targeted neighborhoods throughout the city.

In *The Interrupters,* Ameena's introduction begins with the revelation that she is the daughter of Jeff Fort, one of Chicago's most notorious gang leaders and that she had also gained a reputation on the streets due to her own involvement in drugs and crime. The film does not describe in detail her pathway to desistance, but one gathers through various poignant scenes that her faith, husband, children, and community all contributed to her transformation and effectiveness as a violence interrupter. Ameena's portrayal in *The Interrupters* sparked my curiosity about whether there were other female violence interrupters like her and the ways in which their stories were similar or different. I was particularly interested in what could be learned about their work as violence interrupters and the relationship between their work and their pathways to desistance.

I met Ameena by chance at a peace circle about a month after I started this research project. When we met, she was all that she appeared to be in the film, feisty, tender-hearted, caring, full of compassionate tears and an indelible strength. Although she was not a direct participant in this study, since she no longer worked for CeaseFire, indirectly her inspiration guided my questions and commitment to telling "herstory" or in this case the story of female violence interrupters, who are transforming their lives and the lives of others.

First and foremost, I thank Ameena, and the women featured in this book, who have committed to a life free of crime while being fearlessly dedicated to their work as violence interrupters. I am especially appreciative to each of these women for sharing their stories with me and inviting me into their lives. From each of them, I learned so much more about life, our interconnectedness, faith, and the depths of the human spirit than what can be encompassed in this book, and for that I am eternally grateful.

My sincere appreciation also goes to Tio Hardiman and the CeaseFire Illinois site program directors who granted me permission to conduct the research project and offered their support and kind consideration throughout the process. Additionally, to all of the faith-based organizational leaders that participated in the study, your willing participation added an important dimension to the women's stories that I hope will help to enrich knowledge about the critical role of community organizations in enabling individuals to live a life free of crime..

I thank my editors at Lexington Books at Rowman & Littlefield Publishing Group, Sarah Craig, Joseph Parry, and Brighid Stone for their hard work and dedication to this project. I had been warned by wary authors about the stress I was to anticipate at various points in the process, but theirs was not my experience. The editors at Lexington Books were readily available to walk me through every step of the publication process with clear instructions, thoughtful feedback, and timely suggestions. For their unwavering support, I am truly grateful.

From the inception to the completion of this book, I have had the benefit of good friends, family, and colleagues who kept me immersed in encouragement. Some like Philip Aka, Sunday Iyare, Chris Moore, Hal Pepinsky, Julian Roberts, Doug Thomson, and Larry Tifft generously gave of their time by reading early drafts of chapters. I offer each of them my sincere appreciation. Other encouragement came from my former Northwestern mentor Dan Lewis and colleague Shadd Maruna, both of whom I owe lunch (on a sunny day, preferably somewhere without hills and close to parking). To Payton, Adnan, Sharon, Serena, Daris, Will, and Agber, thank you for believing.

Chapter 1

The Lens

When Bianca[1] was nine, a friend who had an ailing parent introduced her to prescription pain killers. By the age of 17, Bianca was addicted to heroin. She would spend the next 36 years of her life involved with gangs, selling drugs, and committing a variety of crimes to feed her habit and survive. Her life of crime resulted in over 100 arrests including gun possession and seven prison sentences. If we were to predict the outcome of this story we might anticipate that the future chapters of Bianca's story would likely duplicate those that preceded them. Unmet economic, behavioral, social and psychological issues and the resulting cycle of crime that characterized Bianca's prior existence would continue to be met with the revolving door of the criminal justice system until the door closes for life or a life is lost.

Stories like Bianca's contribute to the use of the metaphor of a revolving door to describe the prison system in America as a constant stream of offenders seemingly return to correctional institutions as soon as they are released. Over the past three decades, the rate of incarceration in the United States has more than quadrupled, earning the United States the distinction of having the world's highest incarceration rate of 716 per 100,000 people and 2.2 million people in prison or jail (Walmsley, 2013). The total U.S. state and federal prison population alone in 2012 was 1,570,400, and of the 95 percent that are expected to be released and return to their communities, approximately 40 percent are predicted to recidivate within 3 years.[2] The recycling of persons in and out of the criminal justice system has too long been accepted as our best option to address crime and the conditions that contribute to criminal behavior. Perceptions of the criminal as flawed, abnormal, predatory, and undeserving based upon their poor decision making and personal inadequacies, and assumptions that the State through the criminal justice system is efficiently, effectively, and adequately utilizing our tax dollars to combat crime, are all compelling factors that justify our response (or lack thereof) to crime, but is our response just?

These prevailing perceptions and assumptions about crime and crime control contribute to the anticipation of a dismal outcome for Bianca, yet her story has an unexpected ending. After serving her last prison sentence, Bianca was released into dire circumstances characterized by poverty, unemployment, and exposure to drugs and crime, and when faced with homelessness, she desperately sought and found refuge in a community-based organization that provided transitional housing and supportive services. Here she developed a supportive relationship with staff members who then exposed her to opportunities to participate in community outreach, organizing, advocacy, leadership, and employment-related activities. Within 18 months after her release from prison, Bianca had attended the President of the United States Barack Obama's second inaugural ball and risen from outreach worker to supervisor as an esteemed and paid employee in a crime prevention and conflict resolution organization in one of Chicago's toughest neighborhoods. In this neighborhood, children, gang members, and others whom she has literally shielded from a bullet or helped to avoid a life leading to incarceration or death, call her "Mama."

Bianca's transformation was not an accident of fate. Although she is exceptional, she is not the exception. Bianca is exceptional in that she was willing not to allow her notions of self to be circumscribed by the pressures of prevailing perceptions and assumptions that failed to acknowledge the worth of her potential contributions to the well-being of others, yet others like her with criminal histories and untapped potential have also experienced a similar transformation when their agency, impetus for change, and desire to positively contribute to society are matched with opportunity and support within communities of care.

At some point, the majority of those who are imprisoned will be released. While multiple systems encounter individuals on the pathway to incarceration, not one system exists with the specific function to provide a pathway out. Like Bianca, those that are released tend to return to communities challenged by high rates of violence, crime, unemployment, and poverty. In these conditions, without some type of intervention, they are likely to reoffend. This book, through compelling interviews and field research with formerly gang-affiliated women, illuminates how with community support provided by faith-based organizations and their active engagement in peace-oriented work in distressed communities throughout Chicago the women were able to desist from crime, rebuild their lives, and become meaningful contributors to the well-being of troubled children, youth, and adults in their communities.

The stories of transformation from the women in this book are not isolated anecdotal coincidences. The reconstruction that has occurred in their lives, like Bianca's, is the result of intentional change efforts facilitated within communities of care, and therefore, these efforts can be replicated, systematized, institutionalized, supported, and promoted as standard policy and practice. Given general public sentiment and fear of crime since the onset of the war on crime and drugs the 1980s, few politicians would have been likely to win elections by appearing to be soft on crime, yet the halo effect that has stifled opposition to the tactics used to support this war is fading as both liberals and conservatives have launched criticism about its failures. Liberals attribute the disconcerting outcome of an overburdened criminal justice system to harsh and rigid, and some have said racist, sentencing laws coupled with heavy handed policing, while conservatives are distressed about the overwhelming cost of maintaining the prison industrial complex amidst local, state, and federal budgetary crises. Collective concerns about the state of the current criminal justice system have sowed the seeds of bipartisan political will and contributed to the development of favorable conditions for pursuing discussions about alternatives including diversion and early release for nonviolent criminals.

The criminal justice system consists of the corrections, judicial, and penal systems that function to arrest, prosecute, and incarcerate those that are caught committing a crime. Not every person who leaves a store knowing that not every item in their bag was paid for, has been in a physical altercation, has drank too much alcohol and got behind a wheel to drive, possessed marijuana, or engaged in any other criminal activity has got caught, and some persons are more likely to get caught than others. For those that become involved in the criminal justice system, the troubling fact is that while multiple systems exist to stigmatize, indict, and isolate them from society, comparable investment in systems and resources to facilitate their reentry and commitment to desist from crime does not exist.

The officers that are responsible for the parole process as a component of the criminal justice system tend to be overburdened with extremely high caseloads that in addition to supervision require corresponding paperwork and administrative duties. They perform these duties in a context where they have less resources and support to facilitate the reentry and desistance processes than they do to enforce the re-incarceration of their clients. The lack of resources dedicated to the desistance and reentry processes leads to a situation where rather than seeking out their parole officers for support, according to a parole officer, "when they (parolees) see us (parole officers) on the street, they scatter." This state of affairs is not indicative of the failed attributes of the officers or parolees alone, but of the lack of a formal system of supports to facilitate the reentry and desistance processes. Missing in the criminal justice system is a legislated mandate, dedicated funding, formal administrative processes, standardized operating procedures, policies, and protocol, and adequate staffing including public, private, and community-based support to facilitate desistance from crime during reentry.

The stories of the women in this study point to the need for innovative approaches for equipping "desisters," persons who have made a decision to refrain from a criminal lifestyle (Maruna, 2001), with the human and social capital these individuals need to maintain their commitment to abstain from crime and contribute meaningfully to their communities and society at large. Together their experiences challenge deep-rooted assumptions that are aligned with perspectives that support a retributive (punitive) criminal justice system that does little to equip persons with the networks, tools, opportunities, and resources needed to help them to refrain from falling back into a criminal lifestyle once released. Together their voices join others that call for an alternative approach to persons seeking to desist from crime that acknowledges, supports, and mobilizes the inherent assets that all individuals and communities possess to improve their well-being.

TRANSFORMING DISCOURSE ON CRIME AND JUSTICE

Movement toward an alternative response to crime and justice requires challenging a fundamental assumption that underpins the contemporary "war on crime" which is that fear of punishment deters crime. This criminological assumption of deterrence is linked to theories about self-interest which postulate that deviance is a result of the natural inclinations for individuals to both subordinate the needs of others to their own and forfeit delayed gratification in favor of satisfying their short-term needs and desires (Agnew, 2014, p. 2). By viewing crime as a result of self-interest, punishment becomes a normative response and means of deterring crime and deviance.

War is an ultimate form of punishment. The war on crime has included a massive expansion of the prison industrial complex and "get-tough on crime" strategies which have resulted in an exponential increase in incarceration rates since the mid-1990s. Three key components of the war on crime have been mandatory minimum sentencing, three-strikes laws, and "broken windows policing." The mandatory minimum sentencing guidelines limit judicial discretion to recommend sentences below the minimum in criminal cases which increased penalties for drug crimes and limited judicial discretion, such as in considering whether an individual played a minor or major role in the offense. The corresponding three-strikes legislation targets repeat, habitual, or persistent offenders (also referred to as "career criminals") and guarantees their removal from society by requiring anyone convicted of three violent, and in some cases nonviolent, felonies to receive a sentence of 25 years to life.[3]

The lack of opposition to the three-strikes legislation coincided with predictions that the nation would be flooded with a "new breed" of young offenders. DiIulio (1995) labeled these young persons *superpredators* and described them as lacking fathers, God, and jobs, who had "no respect for human life and no sense of the future. . . ." (p. 23). In step with DiIulio, James Q. Wilson (1995) predicted that by the year 2000, the nation would include "thirty thousand more young muggers, killers and thieves than. . . ." (p. 507). Wilson and DiIulio's predictions contributed to prison expansion, an increase in the number of adults and juveniles imprisoned with life sentences, and have spurred the continued pursuit of the war on crime into the new millennium, yet they were horribly wrong. Wilson and DiIulio's predictions of an invasion of kid killers and thieves were grossly false, as instead of the dramatic increase they forecasted, the rate of youth violence has sustained a steep drop since the mid-1990s, (Zimring & Rushin, 2013; Howell, 2009).

Another aspect of the get-tough on crime strategies is "broken windows" policing or "zero tolerance" policing. Both terms refer to tactics derived from an influential article written by James Q. Wilson & George L. Kelling (1982) in which they presented the *broken windows thesis,* the idea that tolerating slight criminal infractions leads to more serious crime.[4] This thesis implies that minor disorders such as loitering, graffiti, public drunkenness, prostitution, and panhandling must be dealt with aggressively through the enforcement of minor misdemeanor laws to deter crime and prevent the pervasive spread of criminal activity, including violent crime, and moral decay throughout communities and society. Broken windows policing promotes the use of stop-and-frisk and other aggressive law enforcement tactics to confront disorderly behavior and target persons acting "suspiciously." Evaluations of the broken windows thesis suggest that the theory is flawed and the associated policing strategies serve to damage the historically fragile relationships that often exist between the police and members of the most disenfranchised communities, typically comprised of low income and impoverished racial and ethnic minorities (Gau & Brunson, 2010; Solis et al. 2009; Weitzer & Brunson, 2009; Reiman, 2003).

Until recently, the war on crime was widely accepted as a successful strategy for creating a safer society. The general decline in overall crime rates in urban areas provides an objective measure of the war's success to proponents, and may suggest that heavy handed policing is an effective means of reducing crime (Bratton, 1999; Kelling, 2000, Kelling & Bratton, 1998). In addition to property crimes, violent crimes in Chicago have generally declined over the past two decades. In 2011, 433 murders were reported, which indicates a significant reduction compared to the 928 homicides reported in 1991, and 508 homicides were reported in 2012.[5] The reduction in overall crime rates including homicides over the past two decades could be acknowledged as further support for the war on crime, except that the homicide rate per capita in Chicago (approximately 19.4 per 100,000) is significantly higher than those of comparable urban metropolises such as New York and Los Angeles (at 6.0 and 7.5 per 100,000 respectively). The alarming rate of homicides in Chicago in comparison to other urban areas and the daily media headlines serve as constant reminders of a "crisis" spurring public outcry for immediate intervention that goes beyond the war on crime as a solution.

The growing opposition and resentment in response to the war on crime has recently included multiethnic and multigenerational protests organized in cities nationwide against the use of excessive force by police and security officers. Mass protests by diverse groups in America in response to the killings of unarmed Black men and boys by law enforcement agents including the widely publicized cases of Trayvon Martin in 2012, and Michael Brown, Eric Garner, and 12-year-old Tamir Rice in 2014, are evidence of the public's growing opposition to the heavy-handed "broken windows" policing and institutionalized racism that is inherent within the criminal justice system. The State's failure to indict representatives of law enforcement in these cases where officers killed unarmed African American men and boys served as a reminder of the persistent trend of injustice and violence perpetrated by the State against Blacks since slavery. Perhaps George Vold was prophetic as in 1958 he described the individual criminal "as essentially a soldier under conditions of warfare: his behavior may not be 'normal' or 'happy' or 'adjusted'—it is the behavior of the soldier doing what is to be done in wartime," (Vold, 1958, p. 309). In the case of the unarmed Black boys and men murdered by law enforcement agents, the conditions of war are apparent, yet defining who the criminal is depends upon one's perspective.

Critics of the war on crime present an evidence that the get-tough strategies have resulted an array of problems with grave social, economic, political ramifications. In 1995, Tonry in *Malign Neglect: Race, Crime, and Punishment in America* called attention to trends that showed the devastating effect of mass incarceration on minority communities as Black and Latinos tend to be disproportionately represented among the country's incarcerated population. Over a decade later in 2010, Michelle Alexander in her book *The New Jim Crow: Mass Incarceration in the Age of Colorblindness* surmised that the costs of the war on drugs and crime continued to outweigh the benefits to society.

Evidence against the war on crime continues to mount as the growth in the population of incarcerated females exceeds that of males. The number of women entering the nation's state and federal prisons between 1980 and 2010 increased by 646 percent compared to a 419 percent increase in the number of men entering prison during that same time period (Calahan, 1986; Guerino et al. 2011). Unmet economic and health issues such as poverty,

HIV, mental health, substance abuse, and physical and sexual violence have paved the pathways to prison for many women (Glaze & Maruschak, 2008; James & Glaze, 2006; Maruschak, 2008; Bonta et al. 1995; Chesney-Lind, 1997; Richie, 2001). While in 2010, black women were three times more likely to be incarcerated than their white counterparts, between 2000 and 2010 the rate of incarceration for white and Hispanic females increased (38 percent and 28 percent respectively) whereas the rate for black females decreased by 35 percent (Guerino et al. 2011). Property offenses, drug offenses, and violent crimes (predominantly assault/battery) represent the most prevalent crimes among female offenders, and a majority of imprisoned women are mothers, with 62 percent having lived with their children prior to incarceration (Women's Prison Association, 2009).

States are also recognizing that increasing the prison population exponentially and incarcerating unprecedented numbers of inmates for life creates an overwhelming fiscal burden. In addition to a bloated mass incarceration system, mandatory sentencing has resulted in an aging population of three-strike offenders serving 25 years to life sentences, some for offenses as petty as stealing a slice of pizza, a bottle of Tylenol, golf clubs or a cell phone (Zimring et al. 2001). The number of persons serving life sentences in prison rose from 34,000 in 1984 to 159,520 in 2012 (Nellis, 2013). During this time State expenditures on corrections also rose from 6.7 billion in 1985 to 53.3 billion in 2012 (National Association of State Budget Officers, 1985–2012).

Concerns about state and federal budget constraints have opened discussions to consider alternative views on mandatory sentencing and three-strikes laws. Budgetary considerations coupled with litigation by advocacy groups claiming the overcrowded prison conditions are a violation of prisoner rights, have contributed to a call to roll back mass incarceration (Jacobson, 2005; Tonry, 2014). The prospects of early release for nonviolent offenders, ending or narrowing the scope of mandatory minimum sentencing for drug offenses, and legalizing marijuana are pressing considerations for policy makers at federal, state, and local levels that have implications for communities to which persons with criminal histories will be either diverted or returned.

Early release would seem to be an ideal resolution to the problem of prison overcrowding if prisoners were returning to communities and situations where they could readily obtain employment, housing, and support that would be conducive to a new life as a law-abiding citizen. Once released the vast majority of the formerly incarcerated return to their communities and are faced with challenges that are inherent in neighborhoods characterized by high levels of social and economic disadvantage and disinvestment (Visher et al. 2004, 2010; La Vigne et al. 2004). The formerly incarcerated are also vulnerable to the stigma associated with a criminal background, the loss of human capital while incarcerated, and the legally and socially sanctioned barriers that limit their job prospects including the revocation of drivers licenses and the denial of public benefits (Hancy, 2002; Harris & Keller, 2005; Thompson & Cummings, 2010; Harm & Phillips, 2001).

When greeted by their communities with a lack of opportunity to demonstrate a legitimate identity as a law-abiding citizen after their release, the formerly incarcerated are likely to reoffend. As a critique to social disorganization theory which states that high rates of poverty, unemployment, economic marginalization, physical decay, and mobility in neighborhoods contribute to crime (Shaw & McKay, 1969), research on collective efficacy and social integration (Agnew, 2014; Sampson & Wikstrom, 2006) suggests that despite these challenges, effective community support within these same neighborhoods can help to provide the formerly incarcerated with the tools to rebuild their lives.

COMMUNITIES AND DESISTANCE: AN ALTERNATIVE

Fostering a shift from the State-led and deterrence-oriented system of criminal justice toward one that is community driven and peace centered would require significant changes not only in standard operations and procedures, but also in the assumptions that drive them. One fundamental ideological change that would be needed is to recognize the interdependence and worth of every individual and community and their potential to offer meaningful contributions to the overall societal well-being.

A foundational tenet of an assets-based approach to change and reform through capacity building is the affirmation of the inherent or potential faculties of worth of all individuals, organizations, and communities. These capacities are inclusive of human capital (skills, behaviors, and knowledge) and social capital (relationships and networks of support) which can be mobilized to enhance their well-being. The assets-based approach is related to "strengths-based" practice in social work which assumes that every individual, group, family, and community has strengths that should be identified, and harvested (Sheafor & Horejsi, 2003, 93; Corcoran, 2008; McMillen, Morris, & Sherraden, 2004; Rapp, 1997; Saleebey, 2005).

When applied to community development and social change initiatives, the assets-based approach acknowledges the resiliency of communities as well as individuals to actuate, in partnership with similarly-minded others, their capabilities and resources for solving their own problems. The work of Kretzmann and McKnight (1996) on assets-based community development highlighted the potential of identifying and mobilizing community assets (human and social capital), despite every obstacle, including economic challenges, that threaten to militate against their best efforts. The assets-based approach is aligned with a philosophy that views individuals and communities as resourceful, resilient, and capable of unlocking and directing their strengths, resources and capabilities toward solving their own problems and overcoming adversity (Saleebey, 2005; Rapp, 1997; McMillen et al. 2004; Corcoran, 2008).

When applied to desistance from crime, rather than crime control, the assets-based approach challenges prevailing policies and practices that support the current criminal justice system by widening the lens beyond a focus on individual deficits of *offenders*. The assets-based approach encompasses a broader environmental view of the problem and potential solutions. By emphasizing and integrating the strengths, resources, or assets within an individual's social environment (such as family and community-based support including social service, faith-based, education, employment, and health sectors), this approach also functions to depathologize individuals and communities by shifting blame for society's ills toward the social structures that impact them (Saleebey, 2005; VanDenBerg, 1996).

What we believe we can and cannot change depends upon our perspective. Our cultural values and world view shape how we think about possibilities and the potential for individual and systemic reform or social change. If there existed a sphere that included all of the possible ways of viewing the world and understanding the nature of society, the consensus and conflict views would be positioned at opposite poles (Blakemore, 2007). Each view has implications for the perpetuation of assumptions about criminality and desired policy responses. The consensus perspective suggests that a lawful and just society is achieved when there is agreement that the duty of community members is to obey the law and the responsibility of the State is to protect their individual rights to freedom and security.[6] The emphasis from the conflict perspective is not on the role of the State in maintaining social protections but the way in which inequality or differential opportunity structures supported by the State not only shape delinquent behavior, but shape social perceptions of and responses to delinquent behavior (Cloward & Ohlin, 1960).[7] The conflict view argues for reform at the micro-, mezzo-, and macro-levels of society through the cultivation of community by building mutual trust and responsibility among citizens as well as the redistribution of power and wealth by the State to reduce crime and foster an equitably shared sense of security and social justice. In between the two extremes of conflict and consensus views are various worldviews that differ by degrees in regard to the extent to which notions of individual freedom or social structural constraints and entitlements are believed to determine differential outcomes. One view that lies between the two extremes is the humanist perspective.

The humanist perspective acknowledges diversity in society and the necessity for the law provide an unbiased means to objectively and peacefully mediate between conflicting groups, resolve disputes, and improve well-being for the greater good of society. To reduce crime, the humanist perspective advocates for the use of practices, including restorative justice, which seek to repair the harm committed and reduce social fragmentation by restoring relationships in society as an alternative to the traditional retributive criminal justice system. This perspective is related to the work of peace activists such as Mahatma Ghandi and worldviews that acknowledge human interdependence. Ubuntu is a South African concept meaning: "I am what I am because of who we are."[8] Humanist worldviews such as Ubuntu acknowledge the interconnectedness of humanity and the futility of trends toward social isolation and individualism. The humanist view blends aspects of the consensus perspective by recognizing the role of the State in providing social protections, and the conflict view by advocating for reform.

The emergence of restorative justice practices within the criminal justice system that engage offenders (persons who harmed), victims (the harmed), and community members in discussions to address and ideally repair the harm caused demonstrates an openness to a humanist approach to change. Restorative justice is defined as an alternative philosophy that views crime as a violation of people and social relationships that must be repaired by addressing the *needs* of victims and offenders, the *obligation* of offenders to repair harm, and the *engagement* of community members in an effort to put things right (Zehr, 2002: 21). The application of restorative justice practices is varied and evolving worldwide, yet the primary focus of restorative justice practices is about addressing the obligation for offenders to "right wrongs" and heal the harm they have caused victims (Pepinsky, 2013; Zehr, 2005).

Underemphasized in restorative justice practice is the intentional facilitation of desistance and reentry, and therefore restorative justice although an essential humanist strategy should not be viewed as a one-size fits all alternative response to all issues related to criminality. In light of the current emphasis on the deinstitutionalization of nonviolent offenders and the repeal and narrowing of sentencing laws, the need for critical thinking about the roles, responsibilities, and possibilities of the State, the community, and individuals (the citizenry) for responding to the needs of persons seeking to desist from crime remains.

Now perhaps more than any time in the recent history of the United States of America, there appears to be a widening of the window of opportunity for changing the discourse on crime and justice away from the deterrence-oriented and State-centered options that led to the war on crime and toward increasingly humanist alternatives. Viable lower-cost and community-based alternatives to incarceration such as restorative justice strategies are receiving increased attention, these types of initiatives remain underfunded, undervalued, fragmented, and marginalized within milieu of programs that are aligned with the dominant retributive ideology that underpins the conventional criminal justice system. The opportunity exists to not only find expedient solutions to prison overcrowding and fiscal constraints, but to shift ideology about the way in which society deals with persons who have engaged in crime. Restorative justice by itself does not address the effects of mass incarceration, respond to increasing numbers of persons returning to troubled communities, or significantly change the retributive discourse on crime and justice. An *expansive, transformative view of restorative justice*[9] broadens the conceptualization of justice to not only involve individuals and community in healing harm caused by a particularly incident, but to address the need for structural change that remedies the conditions that foster crime.

Rather than asking what can be done to wage a war on crime in society, a broad overarching aim of this book is to ask what can be done to foster a more peaceful society and facilitate the reconstruction and transformation of individuals and communities. This question arises from the assumption that steps toward peace are just as efficacious as those toward war, if not more. The answer requires drawing upon the moral sensibilities of individuals, communities, and social institutions to call for an alternative response to crime that acknowledges the contributions of structural factors, such as inequality, on criminality while mobilizing our collective capacities for developing compassionate, community-based, humanist, and transformative solutions that support the sustainability of an individual's commitment to desist from crime.

STEWARDSHIP: THE KEY TO CLOSING THE REVOLVING DOOR

This book is based on the interviews of ten women with criminal histories who were in the process of changing their lives by maintaining a commitment to desist from crime with the support of their communities. All of the women who participated in the study were also working for a crime prevention and conflict resolution organization in Chicago to provide outreach and violence prevention services to residents in troubled communities throughout the city and suburbs. This description of their experiences as crime prevention and peacemaking practitioners who with social support have overcome internal and external challenges related to their own victimization and criminal histories provides a comprehensive view of the potential of this alternative paradigm of community engagement and mutual stewardship as a transformative tool not only for themselves, but for their communities and society at large. This study specifically asks, what factors facilitate the women's commitment to desist from crime?

Central to my analysis is the demonstration of mutual stewardship which I relate to the concept of *universal social concern*. Universal social concern is a demonstrable concern for numerous others including those outside of one's in-group affiliations (family and friends), and is linked to increased knowledge of and cooperation between the members of different groups and a reduction in crime (Agnew, 2014, pp. 18–19). Stewardship may seem to be a distant ideal that is impossible to achieve, yet Agnew (2014) suggests that caring about the welfare of others, the desire for close ties, and the inclination to follow certain moral intuitions are as natural and instinctual within the human psyche as self-interest (Agnew, 2014, p. 5).

Based upon the women's narratives, both internal and external factors related to universal social concern facilitated their commitment to desist from crime. Universal social concern can be viewed as an internal facilitating factor indicated by an individual's demonstration of agency to provide meaningful and caring contributions through their work in peace-oriented interventions in which they risked their lives to prevent crime and violence in troubled communities. Universal social concern is also an external factor that facilitates the women's commitment to desist and is evident in the role of community and specifically, the work of faith-based and other community-based organizations to provide the women with supportive relationships. Stewardship for the women as receivers and givers of universal social concern reinforced their commitment to desist from crime and to their new identity as functional and esteemed community members.

The insight shared in this book would not be possible without the contributions of my informants, the women who shared memories of their experiences as victims, offenders, and now peacemaking practitioners and esteemed community members.[10] The oral histories of these women about their lives and their work can be read as an initial compilation or an overview of the various ways of demonstrating mutual stewardship that are emerging within troubled and highly volatile communities in the United States of America and across the globe. Augmenting their stories are my observations of the work of the churches and other community-based organizations that supported their change processes, and interviews with sources of supportive relationships including the program directors who supervised their work as peacemaking practitioners at CeaseFire Illinois (also known as Cure Violence).

CeaseFire Illinois, an antiviolence program featured in the documentary *The Interrupters* directed by Alex Kotlowitz, is an example of the kind of innovative response to crime and violence that encourages community engagement and stewardship. The need for innovative and effective approaches to violence prevention and reduction in Chicago is evident. The media coverage of incidents, like the January 29, 2013 murder of Hadiya Pendleton, a 15-year-old female African American high school scholar shot in the back, reportedly "only blocks" from President Barack Obama's home in Chicago's Hyde Park neighborhood, contribute to a fear that homicidal incidents happen randomly across the entire city, yet the highest homicide rates tend to be isolated in troubled communities.

Underlying the manifestation of crime and violence within these communities are the structural issues of long-term economic and social disinvestment by the federal, state and local government. In some communities with high crime rates, such as Austin and Auburn Gresham, recent media reports point to school closings, the loss of working-class jobs, the elimination of key public transportation routes, and the exclusion from foreclosure prevention and economic development programs as evidence of systematic and ongoing neighborhood disinvestment (Dumke, 2013; Black, 2014; Jackson, 2013). These indicators of structural violence contribute to the volatile nature of these communities where peer pressure and threats to individual or collective honor and status can quickly erupt into a series of retaliatory exchanges that too often have violent outcomes (Skogan et al. 2009).

The CeaseFire program uses a public health and community outreach model that is based upon a theoretical framework which suggests the immediate causes of violence (norms regarding violent behavior, triggers of violence, and perceived risks and costs of involvement in violence) among the target population can be mitigated through the mobilization of change agents (Skogan et al. 2009). Violence interruption is a process that is exemplified in the work of CeaseFire Illinois which consists of using change agents to identify and prevent impending violence by providing alternatives for resolving disputes. Formed in 1999 and with 15 locations in Chicago and throughout the state of Illinois, CeaseFire programs function in several of Chicago's most troubled communities.[11] An evaluation of the CeaseFire programs in Chicago noted the program's effectiveness in reducing the size and intensity of violent hot spots, shifting gang homicide patterns, and causing a decline in gang involvement in homicide and retaliatory killings (Skogan et al. 2009).

Some of the most valuable employees at CeaseFire (both male and female) include former gang members and the formerly incarcerated. One of the multiple assets these individuals bring to the organization is "street credibility" (a level of status typically gained through prior direct involvement or indirect affiliation with individuals or groups engaged in criminal activities). Their street credibility along with their public health and community outreach training helps to facilitate their social and personal transformation into agents of change within their communities. CeaseFire is one of the few organizations that actively seeks to employ persons with criminal histories. Studies have shown that providing viable employment options for formerly incarcerated persons is a primary factor affecting their reentry success (Bloom et al. 2004; Cobbina, 2010; Lucken & Pointe, 2008; Pogorzelski et al. 2004).

CHANGING THE LENS

Together the testimonies of the women suggest that a cultural reconfiguration is occurring that requires the expansion of consciousness toward an awareness that all have worth, no one is expendable. Their experiences confirm that the intentional spread of universal social concern as a standard practice is possible through ongoing opportunities to develop and demonstrate the moral and social competencies of mutual stewardship and peacemaking. Their stories reveal the contradictions and conundrums for social policy that are embedded in our understanding of the "offender" as a social problem as opposed to a source of empowerment. Their stories juxtapose issues of their own childhood abandonment and neglect with the reality of their function as surrogate mothers, aunts, and sisters for troubled youth. They describe their own experiences as the motivation for their profound compassion and determination not to give up on others who face similar challenges and the way in which the same community inspires them to maintain their commitment to desist.

Howard Zehr in his seminal work *Changing Lenses: A New Focus for Crime and Justice* (1990) confronts assumptions about crime and justice that support a retributive perspective and proposes a restorative lens that acknowledges the crime while seeking to engage communities and churches in responding to the needs of both the victim and the offender as a practical alternative. *Changing Lenses* (1990) represents one of the first attempts to reintroduce the use of a moral prism that blends the themes of community, peace, and interdependence into a humanist perspective from which to view and renegotiate society's response to crime. The process of reforming the social response to crime requires moral compromises and the reconfiguration of fixed traditional or ingrained ideologies, social constructs, and cultural values (such as racism, sexism, and classism) that are difficult to change despite their incongruence and often inherent contradictions within an increasingly plural, dynamic, fluid, and rapidly evolving society.

By sharing the stories of the women in this book, my hope is that knowledge of their experiences of personal change will become less opaque and seemingly exceptional, and as receivers of their testimonies we will become more willing to finding a place for them in our understanding and awareness of the possibilities for alternative approaches to criminal justice that call us to become engaged and responsive stewards. Ideally, their stories will inspire us to expand our circles of care to include others who are seeking to desist from crime. This book echoes the call for *changing lenses,* shifting our collective ideological orientation to acknowledge the potential worth and assets of each and every individual, and specifically those who seek to desist, as the first step toward finding a place for peace in our response to crime.

OVERVIEW OF THE BOOK

The stories of the women in this study point to the need for innovative approaches for equipping "desisters," persons who have made a decision to refrain from a criminal lifestyle, with the human and social capital they need to avoid reoffending and contribute meaningfully to their communities and society at large. Rather than focusing solely on their pathways to crime, Chapter 3 emphasizes the factors leading up to the women's decisions to desist from crime and change their lives including feelings of remorse and regret associated with the loss or separation from a significant other. Centering the discussion on desistance rather than criminality in the lives of the women is intentional and supports the research of others who seek to depathologize individuals and communities that have histories of crime and violence by focusing on their resiliency, strengths, assets, morality, and potential for reform rather than their deficits. Instead of simply supporting what is already known in the pathways to crime literature, the aim of Chapter 3 is to provide a benchmark from which to assess the difference in the lives of the women before and after the point at which they committed to desist and engage in communities of care.

Chapter 4 describes the women's resiliency in their quest to abstain from reoffending and details the ways in which their engagement within communities of care and support inspired them to tap into their strengths, resources, and capacities for growth to build upon and enhance their ability to reach their full potential. Together their experiences challenge deep-rooted assumptions that are aligned with views on crime that support the current retributive (punitive) criminal justice system. Chapter 4 describes how "successful desistance" for the women depended upon them developing effective interpersonal relationship skills, supportive relationships, and resilience in emotionally secure environments. These facilitating factors enabled them to obtain services to meet their needs while confronting, deconstructing, and reconstructing internal processes and meaning around ways of navigating through and adapting to the challenges and adversities in their lives without resorting to crime.

The efficacy of these internal facilitating factors is built upon the fundamental assumption that every individual at any given moment has inherent or potential faculties of worth that are inclusive of human capital (skills, behaviors, and knowledge) and social capital (relationships and networks of support) which can be mobilized to enhance their well-being. This recognition of human dignity and worth of every individual is a guiding principle in social work and community development practice that based upon the women's accounts of their experiences should be incorporated into criminal justice policy and practices as well.

Chapter 5 delves into the role of community organizations, specifically faith-based organizations, in responding to the needs of desisters, by providing them with a sense of empowerment, safety, and belonging as members of a community of care. Interest in the role of churches and other faith-based organizations in working with justice-involved persons has mounted since the establishment of the White House Office of Faith-Based and Community Initiatives in 2001 by former President George W. Bush and extended under the Obama Administration.

Chapter 5 focuses on the demonstration of universal social concern by faith-based and community organizations representatives and justice professionals as external facilitating factors that help to transform communities into safe and empowering places. This chapter includes the results of interviews with and observations of four leaders of the faith-based organizations identified by the women as providing them with critical and ongoing support. Of interest are the similarities and differences in the particular ways that the organizations cultivated community by functioning as sources of empowerment, safety, and belonging for the women. The proposed alternative framework for responding to the needs of desisters recognizes linkages to sources of empowerment, safety, and belonging as critical external (community and structural level) factors that helped to facilitate the women's ability to maintain their commitment to desist.

Chapter 6 provides detailed accounts of how the women in this study seemingly defy human nature, by confronting crime and violence with peace. This chapter features the results of interviews with program managers at CeaseFire about the women's work on the streets of Chicago's toughest neighborhoods. The findings show that programs like CeaseFire Illinois that have provided former offenders with opportunities to meaningfully engage in peacemaking and stewardship through crime and violence prevention in and with the support of their communities not only offer them opportunities for personal redemption, they plant the ideological seeds for the transformation of morality in society. By successfully engaging former offenders in critical roles as leaders, experts, service providers, and instigators of peace, communities help to challenge views that suggest the most effective way to deter crime is through mandated sentencing and heavy handed policing.

Chapter 6 also presents the perceptions of the work of the women as peacemakers and the way in which their contributions to the community function to depathologize ideology about persons with criminal histories. Community-driven prevention, advocacy, empowerment, conflict resolution, and social care strategies that engage former offenders confront perspectives that suggest persons with criminal histories have limited value to society and belong in prison. The stories of the peace-oriented work of women in this study contradict many of the popular images that shape views of persons with criminal histories. The proposed alternative framework derived from their stories also confronts those views by suggesting that persons seeking to desist from crime should be provided with opportunities to demonstrate meaningful stewardship not only as a means for self-redemption, but to transform moral convictions that support systems, policies, and structures that reinforce inequality through discrimination, stigmatization, and marginalization.

Chapter 7 provides recommendations in response to the call for acknowledging the potential of the human spirit and the moral imperative of the citizenry and the State to be co-producers of the policies, communities, and realities they want to see in response to crime. The social, political, technological, and economic challenges and advancements of the twenty-first century have created a context and demand for States that are actively engaged with the citizenry to insure democratic participation in the development of policy choices. Taking time to ground the notion of justice in the experiences of persons seeing to desist from crime is important in shaping the framework to guide decisions and the development of solutions that mark our way forward.

The recommended community-oriented solutions to crime that are aligned with an asset-based approach to desistance are grounded in a Left Realist critical criminological perspective. The aim of Left-Realist solutions is not to rely solely upon State to generate solutions to problems affecting marginalized individuals and groups, but to generate solutions that foster a sense of collective efficacy and social cohesion by valuing the worth and acknowledging the interdependence of all persons in society (Young, 1997). Recommendations are provided that promote the humanist notion of stewardship or universal social concern and the recognition of the assets of persons with criminal histories as underlying assumptions to guide and foster further research and movement toward the development of effective policy responses to crime in the twenty-first century. This final chapter advocates for the transformation of justice by: mobilizing State and community assets and resources to achieve social change and improve well-being; calling for an end to an overreliance solely upon the State for social protections and solutions to problems affecting marginalized individuals and communities; reinforcing the ability of communities to function as human and social capital capacity builders, sources of advocacy and empowerment against social injustice, providers of a sense of safety, basic needs and meaningful opportunities to contribute to the wellbeing of others through stewardship; and by striving to nurture a sense of collective efficacy and social cohesion by acknowledging the dignity, worth, and interdependence of all persons in society.

The next chapter reviews the methodology used to collect and analyze the data for this study. Chapter 2 also provides a justification for the focus on the experiences of women who have desisted from crime, which includes three primary reasons: (1) the rate of female incarceration is outpacing that of males in America; (2) the experiences of the female offender has received less attention in criminological literature than males, and their experiences as "desisters" has also been underemphasized, and (3) my personal desire to take an intersectional approach that is sensitive to the ways in which the power structures and systems of oppression at the family, community, and societal levels work to shape the life experiences of persons socially located at the intersections of multiple vulnerabilities. The use of an intersectional approach to the data collection and analysis was an intentional means to de-emphasize individual pathologies as an explanation for crime and instead focus on the women's resiliency as they navigated through multiple challenges and barriers.

I invite readers to challenge themselves to become increasingly aware of their own perspectives while simultaneously seeking to understand the women's experiences in their own words. This may require moments of reflection to conscientiously avoid the use of pejorative frames or boxes to place the women's experiences and label them as more or less deviant. By opening to the possibility of being affected or changed by their stories, one might begin to understand the ways in which their experiences could be viewed as representative of others who as Howard Becker observed are more "sinned against than sinning," (Becker, 1970, p. 101). I invite the reader to come out of his or her skin and perceptions of privilege and oppression to understand each woman's experience in their quest to desist from crime and change their lives and to consider the potential of a transformative view of justice.

NOTES

1. The name "Bianca" is not a pseudonym. Angalia Bianca, who is known by her last name Bianca, requested that her real name be used in association with her story. All interviewees were given pseudonyms, except those who gave me permission to use their real names.

2. See http://www.bjs.gov/content/reentry/releases.cfm.

3. By 1994, all 50 States had adopted a get-tough stance on crime by enacting the mandatory sentencing laws (see https://www.ncjrs.gov/txtfiles/161839.txt), and by 2004, 26 states had enacted some form of the three-strikes legislation (see http://www.utsandiego.com/news/2013/apr/15/brown-repeals-three-strikes-law-realignment/).

4. For a critique of the broken windows hypothesis, that a correlation exists between the failure to control for minor crimes and the increased likelihood of violent crimes, see Bernard Harcourt and Jens Ludwig (2006).

5. Source: City of Chicago Police Department. (2012). Chicago Murder Analysis Report. Retrieved from: https://portal.chicagopolice.org/portal/page/portal/ClearPath/News/Statistical%20Reports/Index%20Crime%20Statistics.

6. The consensus view holds there is general agreement among a majority of the members of society on what behaviors should be deemed illegal so that criminal law reflects the values, beliefs and opinions of mainstream society and deviants are a minority that can be distinguished lack of conformity to mainstream values and behaviors. Reflected in the consensus perspective are the philosophical views of John Locke. Locke believed that the members of a society should be united in their consent to obey the laws of government, and in response, the government would provide them with social protections. See John Locke, *Two Treatises of Government* (1988).

7. The conflict view holds that the law is a reflection of power relations in society and is used to further the interests of the most powerful which includes denying the disenfranchised access to resources and power. Views on crime that are positioned closest to the conflict polarity are closely aligned with Jean-Jacques Rousseau and George Vold. Rousseau, in contrast to John Locke, argued that freedom is bound or restricted in modern society due to inequality and the unequal distribution of resources which creates conflict between groups in society. In Rousseau's words, "Man is born free, but everywhere he is in chains," (Rousseau, 1946, p. 240).

8. South African Bishop and peace activist Desmond Tutu describes persons with an Ubuntu worldview as being open and affirming of others and possessing a profound appreciation for the interdependence of humanity and understanding of the need to refrain from humiliating, torturing or oppressing others, (Tutu, 1999).

9. See M. Kay Harris in an article by the same name, "An Expansive, Transformative View of Restorative Justice" in *Contemporary Justice Review* (2004), for a comprehensive discussion on the core values of restorative and community justice as they relate to a transformative approach to confronting social injustice.

10. See chapter 2: Methodology, for a justification of the focus on women for this study.

11. CeaseFire Illinois sites are located in the following areas on Chicago's south side: Auburn Gresham, Englewood, Roseland, South Chicago, Chicago Lawn/Southwest and Woodlawn. CeaseFire Illinois' Chicago north side locations are: Humboldt Park/Logan Square, Rogers Park. The Chicago west side locations are in Austin, Little Village, and CeaseFire West which includes North Lawndale. CeaseFire Illinois also has sites in the Chicago suburbs of Cicero and Maywood. CeaseFire Illinois sites in other cities across the state of Illinois consist of those in Decatur, East St. Louis, North Chicago/Waukegan and Rockford.

Chapter 2

Methodology

Using a qualitative design, this study combined an ecological risk and resilience framework to examine contextual factors that influence women's experiences with desistance from crime. Based on Bronfenbrenner's (1979) ecological model, the women's experiences are influenced by individual, family, community, and societal-level systems. The ecological model enabled me to examine the women's challenges, coping strategies, and needs for support at multiple levels. The extent to which protective factors at various levels contributed to the women's resiliency,[1] or the ability to increase competence, maintain their commitment to desist, and thrive in the face of adversity, was also of interest. The protective factors were either internal or external facilitating factors, defined as human processes or supportive systems (respectively) that reduced the negative effects of adversity and fostered the women's adaptation to and development within their existing circumstances.[2]

Adopting this approach, I asked three questions:

1. What are the challenges (risks) faced by the women leading up to their decision to desist from crime?
2. What specific strategies (internal facilitating factors) did the women use to cope with their circumstances after their decision to desist from crime?
3. What support systems (external facilitating factors) helped the women respond more effectively to their circumstances after their decision to desist from crime?

METHODOLOGICAL APPROACH

This ethnographic study rather than testing hypotheses using statistical analysis explores the nature of the particular social phenomena of desistance from crime, by utilizing unstructured data derived from a small number of cases. The analysis of the data involved the interpretation of the meanings and themes through descriptions and explanations of the data. With an understanding of the potential consequences of the ethical decisions and personal values held by me and those studied, prior to gathering data, I sought to build relationships of trust and respect that were not coercive or deceptive (Denzin & Lincoln, 2005). Rather than driving interactions with participants using an information-seeking demeanor, I sought to be sensitive to my role as a researcher and shared my intention to challenge my thinking, biases, and assumptions by being open, quiet, and receptive to their stories in their own words.

As an African American female researcher, my primary bias in terms of this study is my conviction that there is a need to explore alternative and community-driven means of justice toward a more peace-oriented society. I base this conviction on the seminal work of pioneers on the topic (John McKnight, Jody Kretzmann, Howard Zehr, Ruth Morris, M. Kay Harris, Betty Reardon, Larry Tifft, Dennis Sullivan, Richard Quinney, Kay Pranis, and Harold Pepinsky). I was honest and upfront with the former director of CeaseFire Illinois and the others I met about my personal interests and intentions to explore alternatives to the existing criminal justice system and ways to support persons returning to communities. I introduced myself to the people I met, not only as a researcher, but as a person who although not born in Chicago, has spent most of her adult life living and working as a service provider, community organizer, policymaker, and academic throughout the city of Chicago, who is raising sons, and has ideas and hopes for change in the conditions affecting young boys and girls and adults in low-income and high-crime communities.

The methodology utilized a feminist and interpretative approach to the data collection, and analysis of the life stories and reflections of the women in the study (Denzin, 1989; Oakley, 1981; Lynch, 1996; Harding, 2004). The purpose of this approach is to ground the findings in the standpoint of the women interviewed, and ultimately to demystify and humanize their lived experiences and perspectives. The use of a small number of cases involving women was an intentional means of avoiding conundrums inherent in: (1) positivists research that tends to quantify experiences rather than validating nuances, difference, and the production of knowledge based upon an individual case and (2) androcentric approaches that reinforce the "malestream" nature of criminology and often emphasize the experiences of males and omit or misrepresent those of women (Belknap, 2001). The intention of this study was not to ignore men or avoid the rigors of scientific study involving multiple cases but simply to begin with the experiences of women as the unit of analysis. For the purpose of telling their stories, pseudonyms were used in all cases except those where the women requested the use of their real names.

This feminist and interpretive approach to the methodology incorporated an intersectional framework for analysis, which takes into account the impact of interrelated power structures and systems of oppression that blend to shape and constrain expressions of identity, social location, experiences, and social realities. An intersectional framework for analysis is becoming increasingly discussed in criminological literature (Baca Zinn & Thornton Dill, 1996; Barak, 1998; Beale, 1995; Belknap, 2007; Britton, 2004; Brown, 2010; Burgess-Proctor, 2006; Potter, 2006; Ritchie, 1996; Wing, 2003). This study is intersectional in that my aims are to intentionally: (1) place women at the center of intellectual inquiry, (2) blur the social, cultural, historical, and biological boundaries that shape the discourse on women's experiences in crime, (3) understand the interconnections and overlapping influences of not only race, class, and gender, but other factors such as supportive relationships that shape the experiences of women, and (4) apply feminist criminological scholarship to practice.

JUSTIFICATION FOR FOCUS ON WOMEN: THE INVISIBLE WOMAN IN HER OWN VOICE

This study intentionally focused on the experiences of women who have desisted from crime for three primary reasons:

1. the rate of female incarceration is outpacing that of males in America,
2. the experiences of the female offender, and the female "desister" has received less attention in criminological literature than males, and
3. my personal desire to take an intersectional approach to studying desistance to crime as a contribution to critical criminological theorizing.

In this book, women who have chosen to desist from crime tell their own stories in their own words in an attempt to place them in a dominant position as producers of knowledge and meaning and active contributors to the discourse on crime and criminal justice. This study seeks to combat what Belknap (2007) refers to as women's invisibility in criminal justice research and challenge what Muraskin (2012) describes as malestream criminological perspectives that place higher value on the male experience. Until recently, women with criminal histories have remained underemphasized within the dominant discourse on crime as their voices have been marginalized and problematized as objects of victimization and abuse or as masculinized, mentally disturbed or otherwise abnormal females in criminal justice literature (Lombroso, 1958, 2004). This study describes the lessons that can be learned from the women's stories of transition from engaging in crime to becoming engaged and caring members of their communities as told in their own words.

INTERVIEWS & OBSERVATION

In November 2012, I sent a letter requesting permission to conduct the study to the then director of CeaseFire Illinois (Cure Violence). After meeting with the director I was invited to attend a meeting with the program directors of all of the CeaseFire Illinois sites to describe and explain the purpose of the proposed study and gain their permission and support. After my brief presentation, the program directors expressed their unanimous support and shared their contact information. I obtained IRB approval in December 2012, and immediately began contacting each program director responsible for one of the fifteen CeaseFire Illinois locations in Chicago and across the state of Illinois to find out if they had female employees working as violence interrupters (including outreach workers and supervisors) at their sites.

Twelve of the fifteen program directors stated that they had female violence interrupters. The twelve program directors that had female violence interrupters at their sites participated in an interview about their perceptions of women as violence interrupters. Of particular interest was measuring the extent to which program directors felt female violence interrupters were equally effective at diffusing conflict as their male counterparts, the skill sets they brought to the job such as Professional Competence including street credibility, communication skills, and the ability to facilitate trust and cooperation and Personal Style including references to passion, empathy, commitment and resourcefulness, and knowledge that may come from their experiences and (perhaps an understanding of oppression or marginalization) as a female. Notes were taken during the interview and expanded into an interview summary describing the professional competence and personal style of the female violence interrupters from the perspective of the program directors at each site. The concept of othermothering was not anticipated, but noted as the theme reoccurred in the interviews with program directors.

After completing their interviews, the twelve program directors were then asked to identify women at their sites that would be willing to participate in the study and share with them the correspondence explaining the purpose of the study with a request for their participation. Of the twelve program directors, five were male and seven were female.

At the time of data collection, CeaseFire Illinois employed nineteen women as violence interrupters (including outreach workers and supervisors)[3] in twelve of its fifteen sites. From the total of nineteen female CeaseFire violence interrupters, ten of the women representing six sites consented to participate in the study. The women were recruited on a voluntary basis, consistent with ethics requirements, via their program managers. Initially all participants were given pseudonyms, and some identifiers such as the specific age and ethnicity of the participants in the study were also omitted in initial drafts to protect their identities. After reviewing the content analysis of their interviews two of the women did not want to remain anonymous and requested to have their real names included in the book, and all women agreed to allow some demographic information to be included in the book (see Table 2.1).

From February 2013 to June 2013, I conducted semi-structured in-depth interviews with the ten selected participants at each woman's CeaseFire program site. Each interview typically lasted between 2–3 hours. The interview structure purposely minimized probes to encourage the participants to discuss issues they believed to be most relevant to their early life experiences, the context leading up to their decision to desist from crime, and the internal and external facilitating factors that helped them to maintain their commitment. The in-depth interview method provided the appropriate means for enabling the participants to speak freely and at length, which resulted in thick or richly detailed data (Geertz, 1973; Jorgensen, 1989).

I audiotape recorded all interviews and took written notes to highlight key phrases or issues, diagram chronology or relationships, and document reflections or questions for clarification. I personally transcribed and coded all

Table 2.1 Profile of Interviewed Female Violence Interrupters

Name	*Age Range*	*Ethnicity*	*Prior Drug Dependency*	*Prior Arrest*	*Prior Gang Affiliation*
Bianca	50–59	Sicilian	Yes	Yes	Yes
Bobbi	20–29	African American	Yes	Yes	Yes
Carleen	20–29	Latina	No	Yes	Yes
Gina	18–19	African American	Yes	Yes	Yes
Janine	30–39	African American	No	Yes	Yes
Julisa	20–29	Latina	Yes	No	Yes
Lynn	50–59	African American	Yes	Yes	Yes
Priscilla	50–59	African American	Yes	Yes	Yes
Renee	40–49	African American	Yes	No	Yes
Rose	40–49	African American	Yes	Yes	Yes

interviews to aid analysis and familiarize myself with key themes and nuances in the data. As the sole investigator for this study, to increase accuracy and avoid bias in the analysis, drafts of the findings and analysis were vetted with study participants multiple times over several months, by phone, email, and in person. The women received no compensation for their participation.

Another unanticipated theme that emerged in the initial analysis was the influence of community faith-based organizations as external facilitating factors on the women's experiences. With the encouragement of study participants, I decided to expand the study to include field observations of the organizations recommended by the some of the women. After obtaining IRB approval, in February 2014 I conducted field observations at four organizations that some of the women stated were instrumental in helping to reinforce their new way of "doing identity" and maintain their commitment to desist. In the case of the three churches that were recommended, Liberation Christian Center, Vida Abundante, and Ambassadors for Christ, I observed church services. In the case of A Safe Haven, a transitional housing center, I participated in a tour of the facility. Phone interviews with the leaders of each of these four organizations were conducted as well to obtain their description of their ministries/work in their own words. Each interview lasted approximately an hour. During the interview I took detailed notes and expanded them into an interview summary which was shared and vetted with each of the four organizational leaders. Together the observations and the interviews contributed to my analysis of the ways in which these organizations empower, engage, and provide a sense of safety to persons with criminal histories that are seeking to change their lives.

DEMOGRAPHICS

At the time of data collection, there were a total of nineteen female violence interrupters at the twelve CeaseFire sites. The majority of the women were reportedly between the ages of 20 and 29 (8), followed by persons age 40–49 (5), and there were three persons that indicated they were in the 30–39 age category and another three that were 50 years old or older. Fourteen of the nineteen violence interrupters were African American, four were Latina, and one was white. Of the nineteen female violence interrupters, fourteen had been formerly convicted of a crime, seven were currently married, fifteen had children, and fifteen identified as gang affiliated (directly or indirectly typically through a family member, boyfriend or spouse). Twelve of the nineteen women were high school graduates, four had attended some college, two were college graduates, and one was completing high school. CeaseFire requires all employees to be high school graduates. The one female who was completing high school had recently started with CeaseFire, and planned to obtain her GED before the end of her 90-day probation period.

Table 2.1 provides a summary of the demographic data for the ten (of the nineteen available) women that elected to be interviewed in the study. All ten of the women who participated in the interviews described themselves as being formerly gang affiliated. All of the women reported committing a drug-related, property, and/or violent offense; committing a violent offense was most prevalent, with six of the ten women reporting committing such an offense. The two women who had never been arrested reported having committed drug, property, and/or violent offenses. Four of the women reported being victims of abuse. Eight of the ten women reported being separated before the age of 18 from their fathers and four reported being separated from their mothers. The cause of separation included family disruption, parental imprisonment, and death.

At the time of data collection, all of the women except Janine had one or more children. All but one had some college education and two were college graduates with Bachelor's degrees. Eight of the women had been working for CeaseFire between two and eight years at the time of data collection.

DATA ANALYSIS

The qualitative data analysis systematically employed procedures to capture themes that emerged from the interviews and field notes. The data were analyzed in three coding stages. The first stage consisted of identifying salient themes from the data and developing subcodes for less salient categories (branches) related to each theme. The second coding stage explored the similar and different ways that the subcategories and relationships between them manifested in the women's stories. The final stage of the coding process identified clearly developed or articulated threads (based upon the depth of the data) connecting the categories defined in stage one and two.

I sought to confirm trustworthiness through prolonged engagement (sharing iterations of the findings with the participants over the course of 2 years), comparing the results of the different sources of interview data and field notes (triangulation), reviewing findings with three persons with community-based expertise in criminal justice and reentry, and two academic peers (peer debriefing). The participants confirmed that the study findings accurately reflected their personal experiences, and peer reviewers agreed that the coding results sufficiently represented the risks and protective or facilitating factors experienced by the women.

NOTES

1. For an expanded discussion of resiliency see Garmezy's chapter "Risk and resilience" in Funder, Park, Tomlinson-Keasey and Widaman (eds.), *Studying lives through time: Personality and development.* (1993).

2. For further discussion on protective factors and positive social development see Vanderbilt-Adriance and Shaw (2008). Protective factors and the development of resilience in the context of neighborhood disadvantage. *Journal of Abnormal Child Psychology*, 36(6), 887–901.

3. Violence interrupters are trained to work on the street to intervene and mediate conflicts between disputing individuals and groups for the purpose of curtailing the cyclical threat of retaliatory violence. Outreach workers provide clients with support, advocacy, and linkages to a range of services and activities to encourage crime prevention and reduce the likelihood of retaliation. Supervisors are former violence interrupters or outreach workers who are responsible for providing front-line management and administrative oversight in addition to modeling outreach and violence interruption services to workers at their sites. All three types of workers were included in the study, and as a group are referred to as "violence interrupters."

Chapter 3

Pathways to Desistance

Priscilla[1] credits hanging out with her cousins and smoking marijuana at the age of 11 with "the first thing and worst mistake I ever made in my life." Priscilla's story is similar to those of the other women in that doing drugs and hanging out with friends or family that do drugs opened the door to a whirlwind of delinquency. Priscilla explains, "From that point, I went downhill. I began smoking a little bit more and more. Then I got the mindset that I no longer had the desire to go to school and dropped out of high school."

"Wasted" is the word Priscilla used to sum up her attempts to reach out to drug treatment centers to stop her marijuana habit when she was 17 years old. "They told me marijuana was not considered a drug of habit. It was sad." Sadder than the widespread acceptance of marijuana use was its seemingly overwhelming omnipresence in her community. "Everywhere I looked everybody had it. Sometimes when I didn't have any money, I would just go out in the neighborhood and get it."

Marijuana use opened the gateway to other forms of crime and deviance, and in time Priscilla was incarcerated. She explains, "As time went on I met new people and went different places doing different things and was introduced to new stuff, and I was out there for 35 years. My lifestyle cost me 6 years in the state penitentiary, and 15 months in the cook county jail waiting on the trial. And the day of the trial, the judge in 30 seconds told me I was given 6 years, and the bailiffs whipped me around and took me out."

Pathways research suggests that a woman's journey to crime and delinquency often begins with a confluence of personal circumstances and cultural norms such as dysfunctional personal attributes and a lack of self-control in favor of the immediate gratification of self-interests (Oselin, 2014; Austin, 2001; Moffitt & Caspi, 2001). Priscilla's story would seem to support these findings, yet rather than attributing these circumstances to personal or cultural pathologies, there is a growing number of academic studies that view these issues as the result of multiple intersecting vulnerabilities and adversities that color and circumscribe the lives of women (particularly low-income women) with criminal histories (Belknap, 2001; Bernard, 2014; Britton, 2004; Brown & Ross, 2010; Burgess-Proctor, 2006; Potter, 2006; Wing, 2003). Marginalization from conventional institutions, disrupted and abusive family and personal relationships, and institutionalized racism, sexism and economic disadvantage have all been explored as feminist criminological explanations for the involvement of women in crime (Chesney-Lind, 1986, 1997; Owen, 1998; Broidy & Agnew, 1997; Daly & Chesney-Lind, 1988; Richie, 2004; DeKeseredy & Perry, 2006; Maidment, 2006b; Carlen, 1985).

The need to ground theorizing about women's criminality in an understanding of intersecting identities that emerge from cross-cutting systems of oppression has been emphasized in seminal Black and multiracial feminist and criminological analyses (Gordon, 1987; King, 1988; Kelly, 1994; Daly & Stephens, 1995; Beale, 1995; Richie, 1996; Baca Zinn & Thorton Dill, 1996; Barak, 1998; Collins, 2000). Highlighted in these studies is the overlapping influence or intersectionality of multiple forms of structural subjugation such as ingrained racism, sexism, economic disadvantage, exploitation and the historical undervaluation of women on their experiences and outcomes in society.

Collins (2000) describes this intersectionality as functioning within matrices of domination that represent amalgamations of micro- through macro-level power structures and interrelated systems of oppression. The specific ways in which these power structures are constructed and systems of oppression are blended create different kinds of social realities, identities and experiences depending upon one's social location. One's social location can be defined as a unique expression of privilege and oppression based on race, ethnicity, gender, nationality, class, and other socially ascribed attributes. From the intersectional view of criminality, the lens for analyzing the experiences of persons with criminal histories highlights the impact of structural factors on their criminality rather than their personal deficits and challenges perceptions.

AN INTERSECTIONAL APPROACH TO EXPLAINING DESISTANCE

This chapter applies an intersectional approach to analyzing the women's stories by intentionally acknowledging the underlying influence of structural factors on the circumstances that are faced by marginalized women. An intersectional explanation of criminality de-emphasizes individual strain, frustrations, and pathologies and instead analyzes the ways in which the manifestation of power structures and systems of oppression at the family, community, and societal levels work to circumscribe and constrain the life experiences of persons socially located at the intersections of multiple vulnerabilities (Belknap 2001). This new approach to studying crime can be applied to both males and females and accounts for the impact of race, class, gender, sexuality and other risk and protective factors that are influenced by the social structures that shape and are shaped by individuals and society (p. 469). An intersectional approach to explaining criminality is aligned with critical theorizing on how individuals produce unique biographical solutions to systemic or structural contradictions and inequalities, that can be viewed as practical responses to the opportunities, risks, and constraints in society that are related to one's social location (Beck, 1992; Carlen, 1988; Messerschmidt, 1993; Bernard, 2014; Bauman, 2000).

Rather than viewing the adversities faced by the women as a confluence of personal and cultural pathologies that contributed to their pathways to crime, my aim is to acknowledge these vulnerabilities as a manifestation of the women's unique social locations that are shaped by social structures. Their vulnerabilities are acknowledged as persistent factors that result from relatively constant structural influences on the women's lives before and after their commitment to desist that affect their means for expressing or *doing identity*.

Doing identity can be described as a process of navigating through multiple vulnerabilities by engaging in adaptive responses that are more or less legitimate depending upon the context.[2] In some contexts, crime and other forms of deviance may be viewed as a legitimate means of doing identity. Whereas cultural deviance theoretical perspectives argue that crime results from values, attitudes, and beliefs that are reinforced through social norms and interpersonal exchanges with deviant peers and associates,[3] an intersectional analysis acknowledges that the decision to engage in crime is significantly influenced by an individual's social location and the associated vulnerabilities.

Ideally behavioral change (or modifications in the way in which individuals *do identity*) would result from structural changes that reduce vulnerabilities and increase opportunities that enable prosocial adaptive responses, yet in the case of these women, in the absence of structural change they pieced together resources and support that reinforced their desire to change the way in which they were *doing identity*, despite their social location and associated vulnerabilities. Ideally the primary goal of a responsive social policy intervention to reduce crime and support persons seeking to refrain from reoffending would be to eliminate all forms of institutionalized discrimination and structural inequality based on gender, race, and class. Despite the absence of this type of systemic intention, these women were able to navigate through multiple challenges to craft and obtain opportunities to achieve and maintain a commitment to desist.

Desistance can be defined as "the long-term abstinence from crime among individuals who had previously engaged in persistent patterns of criminal offending," (Maruna, 2001, 26). Desistance is a choice that is preceded by risk factors that contribute to criminality, or the engagement in criminal behavior, yet this decision is also succeeded by protective factors that support a commitment to abstain from reoffending. Desistance is also a process in which persons continuously reinforce and sustain their decisions to abstain from crime over time.

The next chapter describes the *interventions* and *support* experienced by the women that facilitated their desistance processes and have enabled them to reconstruct and reinforce a new way of *doing identity*. However, in order to fully understand their desistance processes, it is important to first examine their experience of risk factors and how they may have contributed to their development and ways of doing identity up to the point of committing to desist. This chapter discusses the women's pathways to desistance, and, rather than focusing on the specific crimes they committed, describes the ways in which they sought to navigate through and cope with multiple vulnerabilities and related experiences that preceded their commitment to desist.

CONTEXTUALIZING CRIME: ADAPTATIONS TO RISK & TRAUMA

The women in this study shared detailed descriptions of their pathways to desistance. Their stories included descriptions of traumatic experiences that contextualized the crime and delinquency that followed as rational adaptations to their conditions. Their accounts support the results of previous research that found experiences of childhood and adolescent adversities such as dysfunctional and abusive relationships, parental absenteeism and neglect, poverty, and substance abuse were associated with female crime and delinquency (Bowles et al. 2012; Eitle & Turner, 2002; Turner et al. 2006; Turner & Lloyd, 1999).

Like Priscilla, in telling their stories, the women tended to begin with a description of their involvement with drugs as spiraling them toward increased involvement in delinquent and criminal activity, yet further exploration of their narratives also revealed that preceding their substance abuse were the traumatic effects of multiple vulnerabilities. Victimization and trauma are root causes of self-medicating behavior or drug use (Salisbury & Van Voorhis, 2009). The women's traumatic experiences of parental abandonment, neglect, parental imprisonment, and parental death, or death of a loved one have also been found to be prevalent among delinquent females (Belknap & Holsinger, 2006; DeHart, 2008, 2009; Bowles et al. 2012; Bloom et al. 2005).

Gina, at the age of 19 is a ward of the State and has been involved with the State of Illinois Department of Children and Family Services (DCFS) for 14 years. She described the trauma of her childhood using language possibly adopted from multiple and lengthy encounters with corrections, psychology, and human service professionals:

> I became involved with DCFS basically due to neglect. I have had open cases with DCFS since I was five, but I officially was brought into the system at the age of 15. I had been in and out of residential centers and then the psych ward. The last time I ended up at the psych ward. They released me to DCFS, and I was taken out of the care of my father, but he did not actually have custody of me for that long, because he had custody of me through my mother. She lost custody of me, but the whole time he had custody of me, about two years, I was either in hospitals or residential homes. I have anger issues, batteries, substance abuse, and a background of suicide ideation stemming from things in my childhood.

Gina stated that she would prefer not to provide further details about the circumstances of her childhood or her parents' neglect.

Father's absence has been identified as a significant predictor of recidivism (Barrett et al. 2010). Rather than abandonment, some of the women recounted stories about the impact of the death and incarceration of their fathers on their early development. Janine recalled being raised by her father and the traumatic effect of his death on her life, stating "When my father died of a serious illness, I had to take care of me. The streets raised me - older people, gangsters, pimps raised me." Carleen described how she also became involved with delinquent activities after her father's incarceration:

> I was going in and out of the Audy Home (a juvenile detention center) since I was 13. At school I was a little on the wild side. My father had been arrested. He was sentenced to 10 years in prison, and I was having hard time dealing with that. I was just hanging out with my older brother's and sister's friends - hanging out with older kids. I grew up going back in forth from this neighborhood. I had an aunt and uncle that lived over here in this neighborhood, and my mother lived (in another neighborhood), and I was living between them.

Fortunately Carleen, unlike Janine, had the opportunity to actively engage with her father and witness the significance of his contributions to her life and family since his release:

> My father was incarcerated, but he's out now doing fine. He's old man now. He's old and he's a wonderful person. I think that's what affected me so much, his loss, his absence, but he is living. He is not dead so that makes me feel good. He is still making a great contribution to our family.

During the interview other than briefly recounting her mother's address as one of the many places she grew up, Carleen offered no further information about her mother.

The lack of stability and trauma other women experienced in childhood was often attributed to the absence of, or weak-bonds with, their mothers. These findings confirmed those of previous work that associated having "weak-bonds to mother" with female delinquency (Kerpelman & Smith-Adcock, 2005). Bianca who was raised by her paternal grandmother recalls, "My mom left me and my sister when I was five years old." She describes her grandmother as being well intentioned, but unable to prevent her from joining her peers in the use of prescription drugs at the age of nine. Bianca stated, "My grandma spoiled me and never had any authority over me. She let me get away with anything."

Like Bianca, Julisa also stated, "My mother never had any authority over me." While in her mother's care, Julisa was a victim of sexual abuse by her stepfather from the age of 5 until the age of 9. Research consistently reveals that a majority of incarcerated females have experienced physical, verbal, and sexual abuse (Browne et al. 1999; Gilfus, 1992; Richie, 1996; Fagan, 2001; Belknap & Holsinger, 2006; Zahn et al. 2010, Bowles et al. 2012). By the age of 13, Julisa had joined a gang and found relationships that functioned as a replacement for an absent father and lack of a bond to her nonauthoritative mother:

> I felt that I was ugly, and that no one loved me, and that I was just stupid. I didn't trust men. I always wanted a father figure, but I just didn't have that, so at 13 I joined a gang. It started by being rebellious in my house. My grades went down. I would talk back to any type of authority figure. I would get into fights. It started to build up and I realized that I just hated people. I hated men, and I was angry at my mother all the time. When I was in the gang the guys there were so nice to me and my (male) cousin was a role model in the gang so everybody was nice to me.

For Julisa, these "role models" and their life as gang members were the only examples and opportunities that were available to her to help her cope with the traumas of her childhood and adolescence, and it was within this context that Julisa sought the stability and support to navigate the contradictions, risks and uncertainty that colored her life.

Patterson (1979) theorized that delinquency is a result of low parental efficacy which is indicated by the inconsistent use of punishment and positive and negative reinforcement by parents on their children. Patterson's research also concluded that due to the lack of support in the administration of positive and negative reinforcement within their homes and communities, poor families and those headed by single parents are more likely to have low parental efficacy. Bobbi also described her mother as lacking authority and specifically "passive" since she did not require Bobbi to work for what she wanted and avoided punishing her except in extreme cases:

> I am like a spoiled kid, you know. I'm 26 now but, at the time when I was like that I was 19, and the word "no" was never in my vocabulary when it comes to my mom. So I was a spoiled kid.

Bobbi explained how she thought her mother's passive approach to parenting prevented her from attempting to navigate through the challenges of becoming self-sufficient.

> I had opportunities to get good jobs before I got locked up. My aunt was a manager at [a fast food restaurant] for a long time, and she was trying and trying and trying, but I wanted to smoke weed. And when I would smoke weed, I would be like, okay, I'm gonna do it, I'm gonna do it, but I kept procrastinating, putting things off saying I am gonna do this and I'm gonna do that, but at the end of the day I was still at my mom's house. I would still ask my mom for money. My mom would buy me shoes. My mom would buy my new coat. My grades are not to par for her to buy no new coat or new shoes. So I had no wants, because I had no needs, and I didn't need to do anything to get the wants. I didn't understand that as a kid, until I really just sat down in prison and thought about it, and I cried. . . . My mom she's like passive, and I used to use that because I know she is passive. I used to have to do like an extremely a lot, a lot for her to say, 'okay, come on,' and get the belt.

Studies that have examined early onset of substance abuse reported a strong correlation with inconsistent parenting styles, parental neglect, and negative parental involvement including parent's substance use (Kiesner et al. 2010; Kaplow et al. 2002; Bahr et al. 1998). Rose stated that after completing her first semester of college she returned home to find that her mother, who had provided her with "a very stable childhood" and raised her in her grandmother's house, was addicted to drugs, and they were on the verge of homelessness.

> I grew up an only child, having everything I thought I wanted. I graduated from high school and went to university. I went off to college, but I had to come home, no money, no funds. After 30 years, my mother had lost her job at the post office, no money, no pension, due to drug addiction. I didn't know, I just

> knew something wasn't right. I knew things were not going on that used to go on. I knew something was wrong but I didn't know what because I had no knowledge of drugs.

In response to her circumstances, Rose began selling drugs:

> So I came home from school. . . and started working at the postal service in a seasonal position, and I started selling drugs, because the lights were off, there was no food in the refrigerator, the roof was leaking, and I never knew anything about living like that. I knew nothing about not having your heat on, and I was working and I knew I had to do something about that. There was a young lady that I met and she was having a lot of money, so I got to know her and got to know what she did, and I then branched off and started on my own. I wouldn't sell to my family members at all, and they got really upset with me.

Not only was Rose's mother addicted to drugs, other respected members of her family were also using. Although she started selling drugs with no experience, Rose described how in time her status changed from being a naïve novice to being "protected":

> My uncle sat me down one day and he said, "Look you want to do this to better the family, pay the bills and get the house back together. Everybody comes to us (him and others in the family) to purchase the drugs for them. It is better that we just give the money to you and purchase the drugs from you to keep the money in the household," and that's what I did. And then I started making a lot of money and people started looking for me. . . . All I was trying to do was pay some bills, get the lights on and the gas on. My mom was on it, my uncle was on it. I have one uncle that is an architect and he got introduced to it and he was working with some rich white folks and they got on it, then my cousins got on it, so everybody was on it, and everybody in the neighborhood would go to them to come to me to get stuff for them. And uh, wow, then one day I was walking on the side of the house and someone stopped me and asked me who was selling the drugs. I told him I was and why, that I came home from school and my mom was on drugs, and I had to pay the bills. And he asked me who was my mom, and I told him, and you know what he said? He said, "She made me who I am today," and I was like, really, she lost her job, threw my education away, and gave all her money to this drug dealer. Then he called his-self giving me a pass, and put the word out on the street nobody is to mess with me.

Rose's criminal activity at her family's insistence resulted in her being sentenced to prison four times for a total of 10 years. For Rose doing identity and coping with the trauma of returning from college to an environment stamped by her mother's substance abuse and that of significant others meant selling drugs to pay the bills and keep her grandmother's home.

Themes associated with parental neglect, abandonment, death, incarceration, lack of efficacy, and parental substance abuse were also woven into accounts of their own addiction. The adaptive responses of the women to their circumstances were characterized by increased involvement in drug-related activities and crimes as well as their own substance abuse. Bianca saw her story as being atypical since, after her mother left, she was raised by her paternal grandmother in what she called "a stable working class neighborhood." She also described her early involvement in drug use as having less of an influence on her subsequent delinquency than her urge to "hang with the bad boys":

> I was raised in a nice neighborhood. Somehow I don't know why because I don't come from a bad neighborhood I don't come from a family of violence or drug addicts. I come from a very old-fashioned Sicilian family, so I don't know I just wanted to hang with the bad boys on the street. I started using drugs and drinking at nine years old. My friend who I went to grade school with, his father was dying of cancer and he was like hey let's try some of his pills (morphine and barbiturates) so it just went from there. By the time I was 17 I was already doing heroin, and I've been struggling with it on and off for 36 years. Through that lifestyle I started hanging around in Humboldt Park, joined a gang and started selling drugs with the . . . brothers, and that was okay with me. I thought that I had a good life. I was having fun I was kicking it in the park and on corners with the guys. . . . I just thank God that at heart I'm not a violent person, and I never hurt anybody, but who knows what could've happened. God spared me, but who knows. I've been arrested for possession of a firearm, carrying a concealed weapon charges, unauthorized use of a weapon and other weapons charges, stuff like that, but you never know what could have happened. I've pointed a gun at someone, but hoping that I never would have to shoot it, but you never know I could've gotten killed. And if warranted, I could have shot, and I could have hurt someone. I think of that, in the few times I had to shoot the gun, I never shot anybody. Thank God I didn't know how to shoot a gun.

Rose recalled that after deciding to sell drugs, she became aware of how many others she knew and respected were using. She lamented that this awareness affected her thoughts about using drugs:

> I wanted to get back in school. . . . I was doing that [drug dealing] and I continued to work [at the postal service]. Once I got everything back on track, eventually I had a lot of friends that I didn't normally have, because I had the drugs. A lot of my friends they were doing drugs and I didn't know about it. They didn't want me to know, but once I started having it my friends let me know, yes I am doing it. And I was like really, you all are getting high, I never knew you was doing this. You know my best friend at prom, I can remember her hiding from me, running from me, on purpose. As we got older, I learned

> the truth, it was because she wanted to do cocaine on prom night. I didn't know anything about drugs, and I was so sad and disappointed that she didn't want to be with me at prom. Then on my 21st birthday, I was giving it [cocaine] all to my friends, and letting all my friends get high. I had never used it. On my 21st birthday, I took one snort of cocaine, and I didn't touch it again until I was 23.

Although her visit home from college was supposed to be "temporary," Rose eventually gave up her dream and began using the drugs she intended to sell. In time, it became necessary for her to commit other crimes to maintain her own addiction:

> When I was 23, I started doing it regularly. I was depressed, looking at my lifestyle, looking at my mom, she's still using, she's stealing from me, and I would get the bill money together and she would steal it. It didn't matter where I would hide it in the house. Then eventually, all my friends coming around and using it. Then I started using it. Then after a while, you know, you can't stay high off your own supply. Eventually, you are going to do more than the money you are bringing back in. So that's when I started forging checks, shoplifting, anything to support my drug habit.

For Julisa, a childhood of abuse was followed by an adolescence of gang involvement with her cousins. She summarizes how these experiences evolved into her eventual substance use:

> We were living with my mother, and my stepfather was gone. He left when I was I believe 14, because I told my mom that he had sexually abused me. So he left. My mom didn't kick him out, he left, and my mom blamed me. I don't know if she even believed me. So that just made me even more angry towards people. I requested to move to South Carolina [with her sister] at some point, because I wanted to get out of the gang and start a new life. I was there for a year, and I was an honor roll student and very obedient. I came back at 15, I missed my gang. I missed speaking my language [Spanish] with my people. I missed that connection that we had. I missed that false love that I felt with them. I started getting high, and doing drugs, and hanging with the gang again, but my cousins were no longer there, but I was already known. . . . I started doing cocaine. Cocaine was my favorite drug. I loved the numbness of it, and how it felt, the adrenaline rush. It felt good.

At fifteen Julisa became pregnant and began living together with the father of her child who was also abusive. She recalled how her substance abuse evolved from cocaine to heroine and resulted in the neglect of her child:

> I got pregnant at 15 and had my son at 16. I stayed off the streets that year and didn't do any drugs. The father of my son was very abusive and kept me isolated

> and he beat me up all the time. . . . He was very controlling and would time me to do my make-up. He would give me 10 minutes or I would have to wash my face and not wear it. He would. . . . He would. . . . [She pauses.] One day he bit my face. Maybe this much of my face [She grabs the flesh of her cheek into the tips of her fingers.] His teeth marks were engraved, and it turned purple, and I was just in my room for weeks, like three weeks, and not coming out. I started retaliating, and it turned into a boxing thing, and I got fed up and left him. . . . I don't know what happened to him. I know he went to jail [after Julisa called the police on him for a subsequent beating], but I never saw him again, and I don't really care either. I continued to be in the gang. I felt free. I continued to do drugs. I did heroine. I remember I just loved drugs. I loved the parties, I loved being out. I was never home. I never took care of my son.

These accounts demonstrate the ways in which the women dealt with the traumatic effects of multiple vulnerabilities associated with their social location. Their birth as females into lower income and working class predominately black and Latino neighborhoods and families exposed them to the trauma associated with sexual and physical abuse, parental neglect, abandonment, death, incarceration and substance use and predisposed the women to the lure of crime and delinquency. This understanding of the effects of multiple vulnerabilities helps to contextualize their adaptive responses leading up to their decisions to engage in crime. Understanding how their vulnerabilities are manifestations not of individual or cultural pathologies, but of adaptations to their social locations, sheds light on the need for support and interventions that help them to heal the effects of trauma while building their capacity to change the way in which they adapt to life's challenges and adversities.

REMORSE & THE DECISION TO DESIST

In their narratives about their pathways to desistance, each of the women described a turning point at which they felt an overwhelming sense of remorse, fear, and grief related to the loss of or separation from a significant other as a result of their incarceration or risk of incarceration. This contemplation of the loss of relationship with a significant other preceded their commitment to abstain from crime and crystalized their desire to change their lives. Prior research tends to link desistance with maturing or aging out of crime, since statistically criminal behavior tends to decline with age (Benson, 2002; Laub and Sampson, 2003; Sampson and Laub, 1993). In this study the women's commitments to desist occurred at ages ranging a span of 40 years, one had only one arrest and was sentenced to only 40 months and another had over 100 arrests and multiple prison sentences, one of which lasted 10 years. The only theme that was shared among all of the women that punctuated their shift to abstaining from crime was that their commitment to desist was preceded by deep reflection, remorse, and a commitment toward positive change. Some of the women described this as a "change of heart" or their "heart just wasn't in it anymore."

Julisa's turning point occurred when she narrowly escaped arrest. She labeled the incident "a miracle":

> My house was the nation house. The nation house is where you have all the meetings, you have parties, and whatever. . . . One day we were partying in the garage and the police showed up. People went flying everywhere, out the windows, everywhere. . . . No one got caught, but what was amazing is that the police searched the whole house, and didn't find anything. People had stuffed drugs in the cracks before they ran, and I even had a gun in my room, and they didn't find anything. I just knew they were going to find the gun, but they didn't and that's when I said I had enough, it is getting too close. I knew that was God. All I could think about was my son.

The death of significant others, particularly while incarcerated, caused some participants to fear their own mortality and deeply regret the loss of time with loved ones. Bianca describes the effect the death of her father and grandmother had on her while she was incarcerated:

> My grandmother, I love her more than anything in the world, she died in 2004. I was in prison at that time, and I took her death real hard. So now fast-forward to 2010. My father died when I was in prison in January 2011. I was so broken up that I thought to myself, 'my whole family is going to die when I'm in prison, and I'm not going to be with them to go to the funeral or the wake. I mean I could have gone to it, but when you go from prison you go when nobody else is there, and you're given about 15 minutes to look at the body, and you are in shackles, and all the guards drag you away. So I don't think I could've left in five or 10 minutes. I would have been trying to climb into the casket of my grandmother. I would've ended up in segregation or in trouble, so I said forget it. So I started thinking about my own mortality, and I was thinking I'm (in my 50's) now. And I'm thinking, 'if you don't change your life, you are going to die alone in the street. You gonna die by yourself.' I'd go years without calling my family and my children, and I thought once the morgue fingerprints me and figures out who I am, no one's going to come get me. My family might have said we haven't seen her in 16 years keep doing whatever you've got to do to her body. She's been gone long ago. And that scared me, and I thought, 'how horrible would that be, to be dead and alone. At least know that you died with your family.'

For some participants, the remorse experienced after the death of a significant other inspired their reflection on the need to reduce the probable risk or likelihood of their own mortality. For others, remorse resulted from their reflections on the time lost with loved ones, particularly their children. Lynn, who has been involved with crime since the age of 11, described the feeling of grief she experienced over missed time with her children during her last incarceration:

> I have been to prison twice, once for violence and once for drugs. The first time didn't change me. The first time that was out of state. When I came home I resumed doing what I was doing. When I was going back the second time the thing that really changed me was my kids, because I had little kids and I thought about my life. I have three children and all I could think about was is this what I wanted my life to be. I already had two class X's [felony convictions], so when I went in that was what was on my mind. When I went in I had a lot of time, and I said I was stupid. All I could think about was my children. I missed them a lot.

The prospect of a life sentence resulting in additional time missed with her children if convicted of another serious criminal offense prevented Lynn from reoffending.

MOTHERHOOD AND DESISTANCE

One of the unanticipated findings this analysis revealed is the extent to which motherhood factored into the women's decisions to commit as well as desist from crime. Of the ten women that were interviewed, eight were mothers. The inability to fulfill what they perceived to be their role as a parent to their children was a significant source of pain and regret for those that were separated from their children during their incarceration. All of the women expressed a sense of solace and redemption as surrogate parents in their work with troubled youth through CeaseFire.

In Priscilla's case, both the pain from the death of one child and the separation from her other children during her incarceration convinced her to change her life:

> I thought I was up there and was walking around like I was somebody when I was out there. Going to the penitentiary, I talked with God and He began to clean me up. . . . God taught me that outside of Jesus I'm nobody. . . . Three months before the time I was to come home, I got a phone call. They said 'I am sorry (Priscilla), your son was murdered in front of your house.'

Priscilla chose not to go to her son's funeral. She described herself at the time as fighting for her life and the lives of her five other children since she was contemplating suicide and knew she could not survive the grief of seeing her son's lifeless body:

> My son was nineteen years old, gunned down in front of my house while I was in the joint. You see the cell walls start closing in on you. It was a struggle just to keep my mind. I was fighting for my life. He had a beautiful heart. It was a few days before he got killed that I was able to speak with them. You know my children was raising themselves. I wasn't born with no silver spoon in my mouth, it's just the opposite. I've been there. I could write a book about wrong choices and decisions. While I was out there for 35 years, my children was raising themselves.

As Priscilla reflected on the time lost with all of her children she noted that her oldest son was just 5 years old when she went to jail, and he was 25 when she was released. She concedes, "That time is gone."

Some of the women specifically sought out opportunities to work with CeaseFire and share their experiences as a way of helping others cope with the loss of a loved one due to crime and violence. After becoming pregnant with her first child, Carleen experienced the death of a close friend. She credits this traumatic event with inspiring her to become involved with CeaseFire:

> For instance victims of crime, when I interact with them I can easily get into their position because I lost a lot of close friends before and it makes you want to really help them out because I feel sympathy for them, whereas before I probably would not have cared.

Similarly, Janine states that after two cousins and her best friend were shot on separate occasions, she sought ways to prevent further violence in her community:

> Before I became involved with CeaseFire I was just on the streets kicking it . . . but there was a lot of violence going on in our community. There was a lot of chaos in the neighborhood. I was the first female violence interrupter. I've seen so much, I am tired. I survived it, and I want to pass it on.

Priscilla described how her son's death and her absence as a mother during her incarceration inspires her work:

> Now today that's why I work with parents. We go to so many funerals. We are losing our children on every hand, our children are being murdered in the street, and we as parents are dropping the ball, and I am the first one to admit where I was wrong. I hurt for the loss of my son.

Some of the women described how her children were the source of their motivation for achieving their goals and their sole inspiration in difficult times. Carleen stated that her son's birth and the death of a friend inspired her to change her life:

> I'm much more responsible more dedicated and more loving of course. I think that's the biggest thing. I am more responsible. I don't hang out with the same friends, but I do see them and we still have a relationship to where we'd talk, but I don't have any problems with them you just have to know how to separate one from the other. . . . [My decision to change my life] came before he was born, when I found out I was pregnant. When I found out I was pregnant with him I mellowed out some. I decided I wanted to change. For me I think it came because my son, I guess you could say he was kind of preplanned, so growing up I always knew if I had a child I would want him to have a good childhood. When I was pregnant I lost someone close. And that's what changed me, it was an instant change. It's kind of strange I can only speak for myself.

Carleen noted that her way of adapting to adversity changed as a result of the death of her friend and the desire to improve conditions in the neighborhood for her son and others:

> I always thought that if something like that would happen I thought I would turn more angry, but for me it made me more understanding and more understanding now of how other victims might feel. When you're a victim of gun violence before I said I would get angry, but now I cannot even think of retaliating because you never know who you're harming and its effects on many people. So it was an instant change. I lost a person to gun violence. Actually have lost several people to gun violence, but that's taken the person I was very close to when I was pregnant, and it affected me a lot. So I began to understand what it felt like to be the victim and I didn't want someone else to have to feel that pain. And it stopped me from wanting to retaliate.

Gina also shared how motherhood affected her decision to "become the change" she would like to see in her community:

> As a woman, as a mother as a person period, I am fed up with everyone out here killing each other. I am fed up with as a woman, and being black, that we are not given chances because of our background, we are not given chances to grow and to better ourselves, because the system defines us because of our past. So it feels good to be someone out there stopping the violence and reaching out my hand and saying we are here. . . . [Being a mother] actually made me more tired of the crime that's been out here than I was before. If we get enough people out here to be fed up and tired, then we wouldn't have to worry about everybody out here just killing each other. Now you just realize there are lives being taken over the littlest things. You come in here and see all these grieving mothers crying, they lost their child. I actually feel for them. Cause I couldn't imagine me losing my son, and I'll be damned if I do. He will be two.

Two of the mothers shared that although their children inspired their decision to desist from criminal activity, after their release from prison they suffered great pains due to their inability to gain custody of their children. Bianca, who is in her 50s, shares the reality of her abandonment of her own children with the young persons she comes in contact with through her work. Her hope is that she can prevent them from engaging in activities that can cause them to be separated from their loved ones and have to live with the regret and remorse that she feels. After her release from prison, Bianca's children had no interest in a relationship with her despite the fact that she had begun to take significant steps toward transforming her life:

> Nobody ever tells you the ugly side [of a life of crime]. So I tell them [young persons engaged in crime] upfront, 'I mean this in the most caring way I need to let you know what's going to happen; if you have children you're going to end up not raising them. I didn't raise my children. It's like one minute you're having fun and the next minute it's not, when the door slams shut on you, when you get five, six, seven years. . . . You'll never go to prom, you'll never ever EVER have a girlfriend, you will never have children, and this is going to be your life, and after a while, guess what your family gives up on you too. They get tired of what you're doing, and if you're lucky you might get a letter once a month.' And sometimes it hits home. . . . I have five kids the two oldest still will not talk with me and my oldest son was always looking out the window when he was eight waiting for a mother that was never going to come home, and I understand he has a lot of resentment, and I cannot change the past. He is a good man and a good father. He works for the railroad and makes good money. I left him since he was in eighth grade, and I'm really proud of him and glad he didn't take after his mother. They say 'he looks like you and talks like you.' Without the drug addiction, I would have been a good mother, and it hurt me badly to walk away from my children, but the drugs owned me. It hurt me badly to know what I've done, and when I would think about it, I would just do more drugs, and I would say 'how could you leave your grandmother she's worried,' and I would just get more high, and I just didn't know how to change it.

Rose also uses the loss of a relationship with her children as a means to encourage young persons she encounters through her work not to make the same mistakes. Rose's children, who are also being raised by a relative, are actively engaged in her life. Rose described how a relationship with her children, even though they do not live with her, inspires her work:

> When they ask me why are you doing this, I say because I love you and I don't want you to make the same mistakes that I did. I have four children. My aunt was raising them and was receiving some money for them. My oldest, my daughter turned 18, and once she turned 18 she didn't want to deal with her, and she came to me when she turned 18. I put some money together and sent my baby off to college. . . . My other children, I see them but they are not living in the same household. I do things for them. I go to their school. I am very active in their lives, but no they are not living with me, except for my daughter when

> she comes home from school. When I was in my drug addiction and got sent off to jail. I had missed them, and then all of a sudden mom doesn't come home, and I couldn't keep putting them through that back and forth. 'Ok, mom's home now, and now ya'll got to come back to me,' and then mom goes back to jail, and now they go back to auntie. Then mom comes home, ok mom, now time to go home. No, I wasn't going to do that. I put them first, and put them where some stability was, because I didn't know any given day, what I may do. They love the work I do, because they are not worried, that one day they are going to get a call and hear that mom's in jail, or get a letter from me saying, I am sorry, I am back in jail. So they don't have that fear, and they love the fact that the kids in the community respect me and wish that I was their mom.

In Priscilla's case, upon her release from prison and in the midst of her despair regarding the death of her oldest son, she was determined to regain custody of her children, after learning that her mother had attempted to adopt them without her consent:

> When my son died, I realized that I had four other children dependent on me. That could have made me bitter. I had to make a decision to live or die. When them doors opened for me, I got out the joint, my own family turned their backs on me, my own mama. Now I remember, when I used to talk to her on the phone she'd say, 'baby we went to church and I prayed for you and all your babies prayed for you too.' You know, you got to be careful what you pray for. You prayed for God to save me, clean me up and for me to be the daughter that you called me to be and wanted me to be, but when I got home, instead my family being proud that God had lifted me up beyond all my obstacles, they started hating on me. I became a threat to them. As the months rolled on, I realized, mama was getting $2000 a month without me. And behind my back, my mama adopted my children without me knowing it permanent adoption. And all that time she had told me that she was going to take care of my children until I got home, but when they offered money, you know the love of money is the root of all evil. No one could tell me, nothing could make me believe that my own mama would do me like that. I became a threat to my family and they hated on me. When I got a job it got worse.

After going to a meeting at the school of one of her children, Priscilla was told by an administrator how to stop the adoption process since the state had failed notify her of the appeal for the adoption while she was incarcerated. She followed the advice and successfully maintained custody of her children.

SUMMARY OF DESISTANCE NARRATIVES

This chapter summarizes the narratives shared by the woman about their pathways leading to the point that they committed to abstain from crime.

Their accounts are shared not for the purpose of examining patterns in their criminality, but to describe their processes for doing identity up to the point that they committed to desist. For these women the process of doing identity that once involved substance abuse and crime was marked by what could be described as a change of heart. This heart-felt need and desire for change was compounded by overwhelming feelings of deep regret and remorse due to the realization of the potential and realities of death, loss, and separation from loved ones. These experiences evolved into a commitment to desist and inspired the women to step out of a life of crime and onto a new path. Their stories also reveal the difficulties of navigating among the array of options that were more or less circumscribed depending upon their social location and associated circumstances at any given point in time, without needed support. For these women change was ignited as an adaptive response to the feelings of profound pain and remorse over the loss of or fear of losing a significant other.

The way in which the self-narratives of the women radically changed before and after the turning points is compelling, supporting the claim that self-narratives are dynamic and therefore theoretically could be modified or "treated" through intervention (Maruna, 2001, p. 39). The point of their commitment to desist represents a shift in the women's capacity to maintain their old narratives (identities) that supported their criminal activities and the meaning they attributed to their lives (Giddens, 1991; Maruna, 2001). At the point of desistance, their meaning of doing identity changed as their prior adaptive responses to their circumstances could no longer shape and guide their behavior. Their adaptive responses to life's challenges prior to desistance could no longer be applied to their new identities as sources for empathy and compassion in their roles as peacemakers in their communities through their work with CeaseFire.

Prior to the point of desistance, missing in the lives of the women were safe spaces in their homes or communities that leveled, controlled, or mitigated the effects of social inequality, risk, and uncertainty in their lives. The women associated the lack of supportive family relationships, particularly in regard to the trauma of sexual abuse and parental absence, including death, and neglect, with their initial involvement in crime, yet with community intervention these issues were unable to restrict the women from exploring opportunities to reconstruct their lives.

The crime and factors that influence criminality leading up to the turning point of desistance comprise only one aspect of the trajectory representing the change processes experienced by the women. On this trajectory, the commitment to desist marks the point of transition to a reconstruction phase in which the women receive critical intervention. This intervention was the amalgamation of community support they garnered that helped to mitigate the effects of their vulnerabilities, maintain their commitment to desist, and facilitate the reconstruction of their ways of doing identity by being of service to others. The next chapter explores the reconstruction phase.

NOTES

1. The name "Priscilla" is not a pseudonym. Priscilla Simes requested that her real name be used in association with her story in this book.
2. See Bernard (2014) for an analysis of the concept of doing identity, and its relationship to Carlen (1988) and Messerschmidt's (1993) perspectives on crime as an adaptive response to societal circumstances experienced by marginalized populations.
3. For further information on cultural deviance theory and the related differential association theory see Sutherland, 1939; Costello, 1997; Matsueda, 1997.

Chapter 4

Reconstruction and Redemptive Opportunities

After her release from prison and returning to the same community characterized by high rates of crime, drugs use, violence, and unemployment, Rose was determined not to repeat the past. In the absence of resources, systems, and services to facilitate her reentry and desistance processes, she grabbed ahold of what support she could find. Rose described the depths of her determination to wrap herself in the shelter of activities that reinforced her commitment to not to reoffend:

> After I was released, all I knew I was going to do whatever it took not to go down that path again. Not to go back to drug usage and not to ever go back to prison in my life. I kept myself around positive people. I got in church and I stayed there daily. I signed up for all different sorts of programs. I was a very active member in my church. . . . People say that there are not resources out there, but it depends on what you put into it.

The concept of doing identity introduced in the previous chapter describes the dynamic internal processes of navigating through life's circumstances to achieve one's goals, where differences in outcomes can be attributed to the impact of the differential intersections of multiple privileges and vulnerabilities that define one's social location including (but not limited to) race, class, and gender. Life's trajectory is rarely smooth and punctuated by change and transition that require adaptive responses. Whereas Merton (1968) described innovation or deviance as one of four adaptive responses to *strain* or a lack of legitimate means to achieved shared cultural goals, I posit that innovation is one of a multitude of adaptive responses or options for doing identity in the *constrained* circumstances that are associated with one's social location.

Doing identity in constrained circumstances includes an array of adaptive responses that fall between two extremes, innovation and reconstruction. Adaptation by reconstruction involves the intentional rejection of an existence circumscribed by the principal environment, relationships, networks, ideologies, interactions, rituals, values, norms, and behaviors that are associated with one's social location. Reconstruction is not what Merton (1968) defines as conformity, since despite the incongruence between the shared goals in society and the institutionalized means to achieve them based on their social location, individuals like the women in this study, rather than adapting to their strained circumstances through innovation or crime, engage in a process of transforming themselves and their environment.

Reconstruction begins at the point of activating their commitment to desist. Doing identity within the reconstruction process requires adopting a new way of being in the world and rearticulating one's purpose, while simultaneously reconstructing a narrative of redemption and transformation of one's *Old Self* and *Old Other* (the influence of family, community, and society in one's circumstances and those of others).

The previous chapter described the inherited spaces or circumstances (social locations) within which the women's expressions of identity evolved. Rooted in these spaces are a blended history of oppressions and vulnerabilities based upon their race, gender, class and other social factors. The women's concepts of doing identity adapted to their perceived opportunities within these circumscribed spaces. The point of desistance marks the beginning of their transition and the activation of their commitment to reconstruct and recreate their identities and notions of real and perceived opportunities within the same or similar environments.

This chapter focuses on this period of reconstruction and the ways in which supportive relationships and the women's work as peacemakers facilitated their progress. Peacemaking work as violence interrupters enabled the women to continually engage in opportunities to redeem their old selves and environments and repurpose their identities as stewards of their communities and society at large. For the women interviewed, the demonstration of universal social concern or stewardship through peacemaking functioned as a means to actively engage in processes to deconstruct, reconstruct, and transform self and other.

DESISTANCE: FACILITATING FACTORS

Research suggests that desistance is a gendered process, with women's "pathways" to crime and their post-release life circumstances being distinct from men (Cobbina, 2010; Bloom et al. 2005; Roberts, 2002). The successful desistance for women depends upon them developing effective interpersonal relationship skills and resilience in emotionally secure environments that enable the women with criminal histories to confront, deconstruct, and reconstruct internal processes and meaning around their past behavior and future choices (O'Brien, 2001; Gaum et al. 2006).

Research on women and reentry also indicates that external facilitating factors such as supportive relationships shape their reintegration processes and outcomes by enhancing their ability to obtain comprehensive services to meet their multiple needs (O'Brien, 2001; Maidment, 2006a; Skeem et al. 2003; Skeem et al. 2007; Cobbina, 2010; Harm & Phillips, 2001; Trottera et al. 2012; Bloom et al. 2004, 2003). The comprehensive service needs of returning females include referrals for temporary housing, employment and job placement assistance, substance abuse and mental health treatment, health care, childcare, transportation, and case management (Bloom et al. 2004; Richie, 2001; Bonta et al. 1995; Chesney-Lind, 1997; Holtfreter & Morash, 2003; Andrews & Bonta, 2003; Hancy, 2002; Harris & Keller, 2005; Thompson & Cummings, 2010; Harm & Phillips, 2001; Travis, 2005). The experiences of women in this study provide insight as to how the supportive relationships and opportunities the women received from faith-based and other community organizations facilitated their commitment to desist from crime and become functional and valued members of their communities.

Even in communities characterized by high rates of crime, poverty, and unemployment, perhaps the greatest assets that can be found by persons seeking to refrain from reoffending are supportive relationships. The supportive relationships that were instrumental to the commitment to desist from crime among the women were found in churches and community service organizations. Justice professionals were at times also effective sources of referrals to churches and community organizations. These supportive relationships provided important linkages to housing and employment opportunities. In some cases, the organizations that provided these supportive relationships functioned as safe spaces for the women to grieve and nourish their esteem by granting them opportunities and roles that continuously reinforced their identities as law-abiding, civically engaged and socially responsible members in their communities.

None of the women reported finding needed support from their close friends and families immediately after their release. In some cases close friends and family members were sympathetic, but lacked the skills or resources needed to support the women through the complex mental, emotional, social, and economic challenges inherent in their desistance processes. In other cases of non-support by friends and family, the women were simply abandoned. Priscilla described the realization that she had been abandoned upon her release from prison:

> My family turned their back on me and my friends let me down. I didn't have nobody that cared about me. All those friends I was kicking it with, no one tore off a piece of paper and sent me a note when I was in the joint, and that made me realize those people I thought I had wasn't there. . . . When I got out my family turned their back on me. I had nothing and no one that I could go to.

Six of the ten women sought refuge in community faith-based organizations that helped them to reconstruct their lives. Those women that found faith-based organizations described them as places that provided needed support and a safe space for them to grieve and reflect upon their past while engaging them in services and activities to keep their minds busy and focused on the change they wanted to make and see in their lives. The faith-based organizations provided a safe place for the women to engage in internal and external processes to facilitate their healing and gain direction in their lives.

Some women became involved in church ministries during their time in prison. Janine, who had been incarcerated only once in her life for a total of four months, stated her first time in prison was enough to convince her that she never wanted to return. She had evaded arrest several times in the past, but after being incarcerated she was determined to change her life. While in prison, Janine was introduced to a church ministry, and became an active member upon her release from prison. Once released from prison, Janine "attended every activity" provided at the church "to stay busy and off the streets."

Like Janine, Priscilla stated that she began receiving support from a prison minister during her incarceration, and she vowed to find his church after her release:

> He [the minister] would come to the county and do ministry a couple of times a week, and I would say, one day when I get out I'm going to find his church, and I am going to go to his church. One day I was at [a grocery store], and I looked and I saw him with his wife, and I went up to them and I said, hey, hey, do you remember me? And he did. He had a tent ministry at the time. So here I am fighting for my life, trying to find myself. My family hates me, I ain't got no friends. I ain't got nobody, nobody except that Jesus that I had when I was in that joint. And I realized that if I didn't find him [the minister] and pick up my relationship with him, that I would die from the inside out. So I told him that whatever you want me to do I'm gonna do. So every day I would work the tent meeting with him. And you know it's the summer time and he would set up this tent in different places, sometimes he would be on 67th, and other times he would be on Cottage Grove, and I would go to all these different places, but that is what kept me.

While family members were not able address the comprehensive needs of the women as they sought to maintain their commitment to desist and reconstruct their lives, in some cases family members were helpful in providing needed linkages to other sources of support. Julisa stated that she began to change her life of drugs and crime after attending church with her cousin:

> I didn't really know God. I remember one time when I was about 16 my counselor at high school asked me a question. He asked me what was my relationship with God? And I was like, what? I was just so confused, like what are you talking about? A relationship with God? Who has that? What is that? I was so confused and that followed in my mind until I understood what that was. I always wondered what did that mean, like can you have a relationship with God? I became Christian when I was 21. My cousin, he found an invitation to a church in the mud, it was in the summer. It was on the ground, and he picked it up, and he was just so thirsty to seek God. He called the pastor and started going there, and he lived with us, and he invited me, and I started going there. God got ahold of me, and I came to love God. I became so passionate over the love of God, the love that God showed me. I fell in love with Christ and ever since then, my life started to change. I became healthier, I lost weight, I became a better mother, and I believe in my heart that he [God] brought me to this job.

In addition to supportive relationships, the work of the women and the opportunity to help heal the trauma and challenges experienced by others in their communities was also a key facilitating factor in their desistance and reconstruction processes.

RECONSTRUCTION AND REPARATIONS

The significance of initiatives like CeaseFire that engage persons with criminal histories in opportunities to provide support to others goes beyond implementing peaceful means to resolve conflict, deflecting cases from the criminal justice system, and defusing potentially violent situations to repairing harm through meaningful service. Research shows the opportunity to be of service to others allows individuals who have committed harm to overcome feelings of shame and move from an egotistical focus on themselves and their situation to an acknowledgment of the needs of others (Holmgren, 1998). Such conciliatory or reparative behavior has also been found to act as a mediator between guilt and self-forgiveness, as these opportunities allow offenders to experience emotions related to an offense and seek to heal and increase harmony within the community (Ahmed & Braithwaite, 2006; Ahmed et al. 2001; Fisher & Exline, 2006; Riek, 2010; Wohl et al. 2010).

Opportunities for reparative action provide both interpersonal and intrapersonal benefits. (Hall & Fincham, 2005; Holmgren, 1998; Woodyatt & Wenzel, 2013). Reparative action such as being of service to others through stewardship and peacemaking practices allows persons with criminal histories to reflect on the effects of the harm caused, show repentance, and begin the process of genuine self-forgiveness and change. Caring for others helps persons with criminal histories to reconstruct their moral identity and remove barriers to self-forgiveness.

The process of self-forgiveness involves not only acknowledging the impact of the harm they committed, but also affirming their transformed moral identity to both their community and themselves. While restorative justice approaches engage the victim or persons harmed and those who caused the harm directly in restorative processes, transformative justice practices do not require the involvement of the victim. In transformative justice processes the community may act as a proxy for the victim, with the goal being to empower those who caused the harm to obtain self and communal forgiveness and acceptance through stewardship with and to others (Morris, 2000).

Engaging in reparative action requires the strategic development and use of emotional intelligence and awareness to affect change in self and other. Violence interruption, conflict resolution and peacemaking are all forms of "emotion work." Emotion work involves the reconstruction of expectations about how individuals, groups or communities should feel about themselves as well as how they should manage and express feelings about their daily encounters within a dominant group, community, or society (Bernard, 2012; Reger, 2004; Hochschild, 1979). Emotion work is necessary for individuals to become conscious or aware of the constraining and enabling factors, both personal and structural, that affect what Berlin (1971) describes as the congruence between one's environment and their ability to exercise their full capacities. Without engaging in the emotion work that challenges their expectations and acceptance of a hegemonic reality, individuals, through their adherence to ascribed behaviors and internalization of inhibitions that shape their public and private lives, may be at risk of acting to reinforce the same social structures and contexts that restrict them. Emotion work, like that provided by the violence interrupters has the potential to transform society by obstructing harmful patterns and scripts, facilitating forgiveness and reparations, and changing one individual, group, organization, and community at a time.

Gina viewed her work as offering her and her colleagues an opportunity to redeem themselves while restoring their communities. She reflects on how they refused to be restricted or defined by their criminal histories:

> We are all here for a reason. We all have things in common with our history. We all have a criminal background, and we all just had troubles in life. I think it is a good idea, because we all basically understand each other at the end of the day. No matter what is the situation, at the end of the day we can all look at

> each other and say that basically we all came from the same background. As a woman, as a mother, as a person, I'm fed up with all the killing. As a woman, being black, and with our background, we are not given chances to grow and better ourselves, because a lot of the time, I believe the system defines us based on our past. So it feels good to actually be out there trying to stop violence and stop anything that is going on that is wrong out there in the community, and just actually being a person who was out there at one time, just reaching out our hands and just letting them know we are here, we here.

Black Feminist activist Pauli Murray is quoted in Collins (2000) as stating "A system of oppression draws much of its strength from the acquiescence of its victims, who have accepted the dominant image of themselves and are paralyzed by a sense of helplessness," (p. 109). The women in this study, through their work as peacemakers, actively engaged in the difficult emotional work required to confront the contradictions within themselves and their environment. This process of challenging constructions of self in response to hegemonic ideologies that label offenders as deficient, helpless, and pathological is similar to the loss of false consciousness (Bart, 1982; Fanon, 1963).

Through their peacemaking work with CeaseFire, the women transformed their ways of doing identity by losing their attachment to false or limited notions of self, their environment, and their potential. Their work contributed to their engagement in consciousness-raising or emotion work for themselves and others and enabled them to accept an alternative reality in which offenders can be peacemakers. Their work as peacemakers enabled them to continually challenge and reconstruct assumptions about their existence and that of others navigating through similar inherited spaces and intersecting oppressions and vulnerabilities.

RECONSTRUCTION AND REDEMPTION AT CEASEFIRE

The work of the women as peacemaking practitioners through CeaseFire also perpetuated the evolution of their new esteemed identities through ongoing redemptive opportunities or meaningful and legitimate daily interactions to prevent crime, often in the same troubled communities where they once engaged in their own criminal behavior. Well documented in the literature on reintegration of the formerly incarcerated into communities is the need for gainful employment, yet the involvement of the women in CeaseFire as outreach workers and violence interrupters provided more than economic incentive to avoid returning to a life of crime. Previous research suggests that offenders who are provided with an opportunity to express remorse and redeem themselves are less likely to recidivate (Umbreit, 1995, 2005; Bonta et al. 2006; Hayes & Daly, 2003; Maxwell & Morris, 2002). Skogan et al. (2009) report that, "CeaseFire provided an important opportunity for its street staff: redemption in communities where they were active as drug dealers, gunners, gang members, and street leaders," (pp. 3–18). CeaseFire as a peacemaking organization provided the women with ongoing redemptive opportunities to express remorse for past criminal behavior by being of service to others.

The women were introduced to CeaseFire in diverse ways. Three of the women, Lynn, Carleen and Janine, were linked to services and employment directly by CeaseFire staff members who were simply "friends" that they had known who would "check on" them periodically. Both stated that their friends who worked for CeaseFire would invite them to CeaseFire events and activities, and after attending regularly eventually their friends encouraged them to apply for a job.

Four of the women were linked to their employment through their churches. In Julisa's case, the pastor at her church was also the program director of a CeaseFire site, and he recommended her for a job as an outreach worker. Once completing the interview process, Julisa was selected for the position. About her job, Julisa states she, "always wanted this kind of job," and described it as an opportunity to use the leadership skills she developed on the streets to help prevent others from engaging in a criminal lifestyle.

In Rose's case, CeaseFire was holding meetings at her church, and while volunteering to do various jobs at her church, she decided to attend a CeaseFire meeting:

> I started to attend a CeaseFire Violence Interrupter meeting they had at the church on Wednesday nights. A couple of weeks went by and I asked the guy if they were hiring and said this is something I would be interested in. And he said, well today just may be your lucky day because someone is no longer there. I took his information, called, set up an appointment, came in, met everyone, and had a brief impromptu interview, and then I had a second interview. And I volunteered for almost about a year, because to be an outreach worker you had to have an automobile and insurance to keep up with your clients, and that's when I started, and I have been an outreach worker for 4 years now.

Renee's church was actively engaged in her community as an established provider of crime prevention and supportive services. Her work with the church provided a seamless link to her role as a violence interrupter:

> We serve the community through different activities. We will put on different events for the children. About 10 years ago the guys would stand on the corner and wait for the school children to come off the bus, and they would jump

> on them. We couldn't allow this to continue to happen, and I say we as the [church]. We would go out and stand on the corners and we would see the young people congregating, and we would go and speak to them, and we would talk to them, and if the regular talking wouldn't work we would tell them, you will not be allowed to stand on this corner and harass people. You just cannot do it, and we will not allow you to do it. In talking to the young people, we were able to understand that there were other things that were underlying their behavior.

Renee expressed a deep sense of empathy for the young persons she encountered in her community. She described how her dedication to helping them address the underlying issues that prevent them from seeing and reaching their potential led to her job as a violence interrupter:

> From my own experiences, I knew they had social issues. They had things going on at home. Problems at school and the reasons why they dropped out of school, or the reason they were standing on the corner is because they had other problems, and as we began to address those other problems, but just caring about the individual and asking what does this individual need and addressing those needs, we began to establish a relationship with the young people. We built up a trust factor, so that if a situation for potential violent outbreak would arise, I was able to walk up to some of the leaders of that episode and pull them to the side and talk to them, and they would intern go back and call the guys off. At one point I could go up to them and say if you want do to this, you have to go through me, so do you feel like hitting Ms. Renee? Now this is the work I do every day for CeaseFire.

In addition to helping Priscilla deal with the depression she suffered due to her son's murder, and her family's abandonment after her release, her church also provided her with a critical linkage to her work—what she describes as her "calling":

> I realize that the more I would come here that the pains for my son don't hurt me no more. I would come here every day and ask, 'what can I do for you God, wash the walls?' He had already showed me that I was in his favor because the pain on my shoulders had been lifted, and I can feel happiness and joy again. So I realized that whatever it is, I am on the right track, and I would come there every morning and ask what do you want me to do, mop the floor, wash the walls and toilet stool, whatever you want me to do, because if that's all I got to do for God to ease the pain, I would do whatever it takes. If I had a billion dollars I would pay it, but I didn't have a billion dollars, so that's why I was here every day, every day. Every service they had I was here. And that's when I meet Minister Adams[1] [a church member who was also a program director at CeaseFire], and I just kept on coming, kept on coming. And one day, I got a call from Minister Adams, and he asked me was I interested in this job. He said I got an interview for you with CeaseFire.

Priscilla stated that she initially questioned, not her ability to do the job, but her worthiness. She described the internal conversation she had to challenge her own false consciousness about her worth:

> Praise and glory, when I got here for the interview, I was looking around at all of these important people, the Commander of the Police Department and all these high class people with briefcases, and I said to myself, what are you doing here? And then the last thing I thought in my mind was, it's God that called you here, and if God called you here, He is the one that qualifies you. Sit your butt down! A few weeks later, I got a call from Minister Adams that I got the job.

To obtain employment with CeaseFire outreach workers and violence interrupters have to complete an interview with a hiring panel. A panel typically involved local representatives including the police, the community-based agency that hosts CeaseFire at their site, clergy, and social service agencies; together these representatives engage in a joint decision-making process to identify the persons that will be hired (Skogan et al. 2009). All of the women who were linked to employment through their churches stated that they continue to be active members of their churches and regularly attend their church services and activities.

THE CRITICAL ROLE OF JUSTICE AND HUMAN SERVICE PROFESSIONALS

While churches played a dominant role in supporting the commitment of the women to desist and reconstruct their lives, justice and human service professionals were also instrumental in providing needed referrals and linkages to resources and employment at CeaseFire. Rose, who had been in prison four times for a total of 10 years, stated that upon her last release, her parole officer referred her to a church to receive a job readiness class:

> All I knew is that I was going to do whatever I had to do not to go down that same path, not to ever return to drug use and not to ever go to jail in my life again, so I kept myself around positive people and got into church. I kept myself busy around the church and became a very active member. My parole agent sent me there for a job readiness class and after the class ended, everybody was running out, and I stayed around doing different things. And they said, why are you hanging around it's time to go, and I just started cleaning up, and before you know it, I was cleaning up and they asked me, can you answer the phones, can you do this, can you do that? So I just made myself a job [volunteering]. It was wonderful.

Bobbi and Gina's parole officers also linked them to services and employment. After serving 6 years in prison, Bobbi's parole agent referred her to a job readiness program at a community-based organization which has an established reputation for innovative grassroots crime prevention and restorative justice programs. After completing a 30-day life skills and job readiness training program where she received classes on resume writing and interviewing skills, Bobbi was placed at CeaseFire in a temporary position to receive further on-the-job training.

Gina, who was interviewed just a few months prior to her emancipation as a ward of the State of Illinois on her 21st birthday, received a referral from her Department of Children and Family Services case worker to the same community-based organization that provided Bobbi's job placement. Like Bobbi, Gina received life skills and job readiness training and a temporary placement for employment at CeaseFire. Although Gina had not been incarcerated as an adult, she had a history of institutionalizations as a juvenile due to substance abuse and battery-related incidents.

Justice professionals do not always provide effective support to those returning to communities post-incarceration. Overwhelming caseloads, administrative burdens, and inadequate resources limit the ability of street-level bureaucrats including parole officers to provide critical support that may reduce the likelihood of reoffending (Lipsky, 2010). At other times, justice and human service professionals may go beyond reasonable expectations to provide intensive support and needed referrals only to find that their clients ignore or fail to respond to their effort and good intentions. Judges also have an opportunity to make vital referrals and linkages to support and resources for offenders. Bianca described how a prior recommendation by a judge that initially failed to prevent her from reoffending eventually saved her life. The story beings with her recollection of the commitment she made to change her life:

> Before I was released I did pray to God, and I said, God, you know that I want to change my life style. Can you please take the taste for drugs and the street life out of my mouth? I had never made that prayer before. . . . Normally when I get out of prison if I have three dollars on me, I will panhandle the other seven on the train on the way to where I'm going to buy a bag of dope

Upon Bianca's release from prison she went to stay with a friend whom she discovered was using drugs when she arrived at her home. Her devastation turned to desperation to leave her friend's home:

> The minute I heard her voice, you know I just knew it. I just knew it. I said to myself, I literally said the words, "bitch, you've fucked up." And then I got a

> sick feeling in my stomach. It made me sick. It wasn't like an exciting feeling, like maybe she's got some dope I can do. It was like, oh my God what are you going to do you cannot stay here. It was like a sick awful feeling, but I had no choice but to stay there for a couple days.

With homelessness as her only other option, Bianca remained at her friend's home and waited for the scheduled visit from her parole officer, with the hope that the officer would respond to her plea for alternative housing. Instead of support, the parole officer encouraged her to remain at her friend's home. Bianca described how she had to resort to her own resourcefulness due to the incompetence of the parole officer:

> The parole officer came and when the parole officer came, I didn't want to bust this girl out and say there's drugs here, but I was like I don't think this is going to work out. They had bugs and it wasn't clean. It's not that all prisons are so clean, but the one that I was at did not have bugs. I was so miserable waiting for three days for the parole agent to come, and then the parole agent didn't want to do paperwork! She said, just stay here you'll be fine. She was telling me crazy stuff. So I said okay.

Determined to avoid past people, places, and things that could lead her back to prison, instead of continuing to room with the only friend who had offered housing but continued to engage in drug use, Bianca contacted a community-based organization (A Safe Haven) that provided transitional housing and support services. Years earlier Bianca had been referred to A Safe Haven by a judge:

> I knew about A Safe Haven because of a judge in the Criminal Courts building in Cook County, a judge named Judge Porter. Originally a couple years prior to that Judge Porter sentenced me to A Safe Haven, and they have a program that if the judge gives you a chance and decides not to send you to prison they can send you to a recovery home situation and you have to go there and abide by their rules. Since I first went there in 2006, it's expanded . . ., and I called the program officer at the [community based organization]. I called her crying, and I told her, I've got to come back. I'm on parole. And she said, call your parole officer, they will help you. And I said, I did and she's telling me to stay here, and I don't want to get high, and I don't want to be here. And I was literally in tears crying. When you're on parole you can't just move without telling somebody. So [the program manager] called the IDOC [the Illinois Department of Corrections] and made the transfer for me, and I got there in 45 minutes. I cut all ties with anybody during the time that I was there.

Bianca became linked to her employment through her work with A Safe Haven. While volunteering to participate in fundraising and other activities for the community-based organization, Bianca began volunteering at peace rallies for CeaseFire before being encouraged to apply for and receiving an initial position as an outreach worker.

PEACEMAKING PRAXIS, MOTHERING, AND OTHERMOTHERING

Their work as peacemaking practitioners reinforced the women's commitment to their children, their communities, and their new esteemed identities as mothers, aunties, sisters, and caretakers of their community's most troubled youths. The women's commitment to their roles did not wane even when faced with the threat and reality of layoffs due to funding limitations. All of the women stated that at times when funding for their positions was not available, they remained committed to their work as volunteers.

Gina stated her work as an outreach worker with troubled youth has changed her life, "It has made me more tired of crime than I was before. I believe if we had more people fed up and tired, more of us would get up and do something, and it would stop." Although when interviewed Gina was just approaching the age of 21, she said she looks at all of her clients as her children, and thinks that her work is not only helping them, but also provides better conditions for her own two-year old son. "I do this work because I don't want to lose my son to this violence."

Under-emphasized in the literature on female criminality is the association between motherhood and the commitment to desist from crime. For the women that were mothers in this study, their children functioned as a tremendous source of encouragement and inspiration to not to reoffend. All mothers, like fathers can choose to forfeit their parental responsibilities for social or economic reasons, yet despite challenges many mothers continue to try to care for their children. Tapping into and reinforcing the dedication of some mothers with criminal histories to their children as a way to decrease recidivism may lead to promising policy and programmatic responses to female criminality.

Carleen also stated that her work and the birth of her son changed her life:

> Ceasefire has changed me in different ways. My involvement with CeaseFire has made me more passionate and more nurturing to others. I have a better understanding of what people are going through what it might be like to live in their shoes. Before I wouldn't have been able to understand. I would've felt that you should have been able to do better. My working at CeaseFire helped me to have a broader perspective. I guess that also came from becoming a mother. Especially having a baby at the age of 21 helped me to be more mothering and patient with people.

Ironically, due to their work, several of the women were referred to as "mama" by persons in the community with whom they had no biological family ties. Kinship terms are often used to describe the establishment of caring familial-type bonds between children and persons other than biological parents, particularly when biological parents are unwilling or unable to provide care (Gibson, 205, p. 281). Parenting by others, or specifically othermothering is a concept that has also described the maternal care given by African American women to offspring that are not biologically related as a survival and cultural preservation mechanism in communities dealing with hostile or oppressive social, economic, and political conditions, such as during slavery (Foster, 1993; Collins, 1990; Danzy & Jackson, 1997; Hirt et al. 2008). Othermothering is the feeling of a sense of duty or obligation of the offspring of other parents, providing mentoring, support, advice and love, and the transmission of human social, and intellectual capital (Hirt et al. 2008). This study showed that the practice of othermothering, while associated with African American women, is not limited by race or to those without a criminal history.

Their status not only as peacemakers, but as a respected "extended family" members provided the women with ongoing meaningful opportunities to reinforce their commitment to their new identities within their communities. Priscilla observed:

> Some of these youth are from broken homes. They don't have no mother or no father, or maybe they had both but they just can get what they need. . . . What good is loving them if we don't tell them and show them? We tell them we love them.

Bobbi stated that she loved her job because she can provide the young persons that she helps on a daily basis with, "the mother figure, big sister, auntie that they never had." Bobbi also observed that she has found it useful to imitate her mother's nonviolent approach to conflict resolution in her work with young people:

> And I don't think it is bad that she did that. I think it is a good thing because it made me into the woman that I am today. The same things she told me when I was growing up, those same things I say to most of the kids that I am out here working with. So many of them don't have role models at home and are looking for leadership on the block, and we are here for them to go to instead of the gangs or bad influences at school. Like me, some of them want help, but they are not ready for the help, but we are here when they are ready.

Similarly, Renee described how she believed that due to her "nurturing approach" she can easily win the heart of troubled young males and females:

> At home they have problems. Mom's on drugs or missing, so they see me as mother, auntie, sister. . . . I give them agape love that is non-judging and unconditional. . . . I have been to court with you, prayed for you, bought clothes and fed you, took you to church. When they see that, their heart becomes more tender and they are more likely to do what we ask.

The need for a mother who loves unconditionally and who saves lives is evident not only by homicide and incarceration rates in troubled communities, but also in the testimonies of their youngest and most vulnerable residents. Bianca recounted an interaction with a young girl who approached her on the street and asked for a business card:

> And the little girl asked if she feels scared even in the middle of the night if she can call me, and I said, yes. And I said, yes, I will be there to help you. So I get a call, and the girl says, Ms. Bianca, it's me. They fighting over here. Somebody's bleeding and the police are coming. I asked, where are you baby? It was a Saturday, and I run over there. I am holding the person up, and got blood all over me and I am holding him up trying to keep him alert until the ambulance comes. And afterward, I am in the park, and the little girl was bragging, so she is telling all her girl peers, I'm the one who called Ms. Bianca, and Ms. Bianca saves people. And I thought oh my God. So cute.

Lynn echoed the commitment expressed by the other women to othermothering and their peacemaking work. Lynn described her redemption as being tied to her work as a peacemaker, and acknowledged that few have the courage to do the work that she does in her community:

> When I was out there, I just kept thinking, I don't have to live my life like this, but then when you get out there is just so much chaos, and so much shooting everywhere and shooting unnecessarily it makes you want to give up. I just kept thinking. These boys have no mama. They don't have nobody. Who is gonna do something? So, like I am here all day long on my block, by myself, because the other people are too afraid to talk to them. Somebody has to step up.

Throughout the analysis themes emerged around the importance of having opportunities for continual redemption through work that provides meaningful and functional roles within the community. Their work as peacemakers provided the women with redemptive opportunities to demonstrate agency toward personal and social transformation by offering meaningful support to community members in need. The reparation of social relationships, as a result of the redemptive opportunities, muted the effects of social structures and ideologies that would have otherwise likely stigmatized, isolated, and discriminated against the women based upon faulty underlying criminological assumptions that devalue the potential and worth of persons with criminal histories.

Through ongoing redemptive opportunities, the women transformed their identities from "offenders" in the traditional retributive paradigm to peacemakers in an alternative justice modality. In this role, they became essential members in the movement to prevent crime and transform their communities. Forgiveness, acceptance, and social integration by the community of the women as surrogate mothers, aunties, and sisters instigated a process of personal and social transformation and cultivated a viable alternative to prevailing ideologies that mandate and encourage social isolation, discrimination, and stigmatization as a response to persons with criminal histories.

The work of the women as violence interrupters and outreach workers (peacemaking practitioners) functioned as ongoing redemptive opportunities that nourished their esteem by providing them with meaningful and functional roles within community. Their work enabled them to reconcile their past by contributing to the transformation of their communities and themselves. The opportunity to work and be accepted in their communities offered redemption and enabled them to transform their perspectives of themselves and others while gaining an understanding of their worth as agents of change within their communities. The possibility for redemption requires community members that are willing to respond to the women and their work as peacemaking practitioners with forgiveness and acceptance of their new identities.

DOING IDENTITY AND DOING JUSTICE

Together, justice professionals, the churches, community-based organizations, and their CeaseFire job sites formed communities of care or safe spaces for the women to grieve and reconstruct their method of doing identity. Together these communities of care provided the women with an abundance of redemptive opportunities that were aligned with their newly reconstructed identities as desisters, peacemakers, othermothers, and meaningfully engaged contributors to the well-being of their communities and society-at-large. Their roles continuously reinforced their commitment to desist and provided them with new opportunities for doing identity within the same or comparable milieu and circumstances that had previously led them to engage in criminal activities.

Their work as peacemakers provided the women with unique redemptive opportunities for doing identity that engendered congruence between their capacities for change and the needs of and opportunities within their environment despite its inherent limitations. With the support of churches, community-based organizations, and justice professionals, doing identity during the reconstructive process meant refraining from resorting to the criminal behavior of their past to deal with the challenges of their environment. The women instead utilized their agency or capacities to demonstrate universal social concern to care for others in need as an adaptive response.

Feminist theorists have suggested that the processes of deconstruction and reconstruction of language, behavior, rituals, and relationships are necessary to effectively confront oppression and transform society (Lorde, 1984; de Beauvoir, 1953; Tong, 1998; hooks, 1984). For the women interviewed, their commitment to refrain from reoffending preceded a period of reconstruction wherein they sought safe spaces in which to grieve and engage in community with others who support their change process. The church and community-based organizations provided safe spaces for the women to move through their own grieving processes, obtain linkages to housing and employment, and participate in ongoing activities that reinforced their commitment to desist and to a new identity as peacemakers. These findings are consistent with the literature on the importance of supportive relationships in facilitating reintegration processes for women (Trottera et al. 2012; Bloom et al. 2004, 2003).

In alignment with the critical-conflict perspective on criminal justice, this study restates the problem of crime by emphasizing desistance and the potential for peacemaking organizations working together with justice professionals, churches, and community-based organizations to create safe spaces and systems/communities of care that facilitate desistance processes. The findings illustrate the potential of an alternative humanist paradigm that rather than viewing persons with criminal histories as helpless, deficient, or pathological "offenders" acknowledges their potential to be essential contributors, esteemed citizens, and community *peacemaking practitioners* that are *doing justice* through personal and community redemption and transformation.

The women's resiliency in their quest to abstain from reoffending facilitated their engagement within communities of care and support that inspired them to tap into their strengths, resources, and capacities for growth to build upon and enhance their ability to reach their full potential. Their successful desistance processes challenge deep-rooted assumptions that are aligned with views on crime that support the current retributive (punitive) criminal justice system. Rather than pointing to their criminal past, their stories call for a moral response by communities, justice systems, and faith-based organizations to provide persons seeking to desist with opportunities to develop effective interpersonal relationship skills, supportive relationships, and resilience in emotionally secure environments. These facilitating factors enabled the women in this study to obtain services to meet their needs while confronting, deconstructing, and reconstructing internal processes and meaning around ways of navigating through and adapting to the challenges and adversities in their lives without resorting to crime.

The efficacy of the proposed alternative framework for responding to the needs of persons seeking to desist from crime is reliant upon the moral imperative for communities, justice systems, and faith-based organizations to accept the fundamental assumption that every individual at any given moment has inherent or potential faculties of worth. Their existing or potential capacities are inclusive of human capital (skills, behaviors, and knowledge) and social capital (relationships and networks of support) which can be mobilized to enhance their well-being.

This chapter described the relationship between the reconstruction process and redemptive opportunities that helped to facilitate desistance among the women in the study. I define redemptive opportunities as the demonstration of universal social concern or meaningful support and care to others in need. I suggest that during the reconstruction process the women, despite their criminal histories, received opportunities to transform their identities by *doing justice* as peacemakers. Their resilience was intricately tied to their work and acceptance within their communities as peacemakers, stewards, or demonstrators of universal social concern. Ideally this type of study would be replicated and expanded to involve more women and men as participants, but to conduct this research would require, more programs that intentionally employ persons with criminal histories as peacemakers. The next chapter delves into the role of community organizations, specifically faith-based organizations in helping to build the women's resilience by providing them with a sense of empowerment, safety and belonging.

NOTE

1. A pseudonym.

Chapter 5

Cultivating Community

Soaring prison populations as well as the subsequent rise in prison exits have become national trends since the mid 1980s. Both trends have resulted in emerging interest in the role of churches in prisoner reentry. In Illinois, where there has been a more than a 500 percent increase in the prison population in the past 30 years, there has been a subsequent jump in prison exits, with the majority of persons returning to urban areas. The number of people released from Illinois state prisons between 2000 and 2003 increased more than 22 percent (from 28,876 to 35,372).[1] In 2006, over 50 percent of the prisoners released from all Illinois prisons returned to the city of Chicago, and in 2014, an estimated 21,000 people will return to Chicago after their release from prison.[2] Often jobless, homeless, and lacking basic skills, few have access to the resources and opportunities they need to maintain a commitment to desist from crime and turn their lives around.

Receiving communities in urban areas tend to be characterized by social, economic and political marginalization. More than half of the persons leaving prisons in Illinois will end up in only 7 of the 77 neighborhoods in Chicago, all of which have relatively high rates of unemployment, poverty, crime.[3] Despite these challenges, within these neighborhoods, assets exist. Persons that are returning to communities throughout the city of Chicago may learn about programs that provide GED preparation, job readiness training, and referrals for employment, housing, and other services, but these programs tend to be under-resourced and lack the scale necessary to meet the diverse needs of the large numbers of persons being released.

This chapter explores the role of community organizations, particularly faith-based organizations in addressing the needs of persons with criminal histories as they seek to desist from crime and reintegrate into their communities. While all of the women in the study reported that their work as peacemakers provided a significant and ongoing source of inspiration and support, six of the women stated that their involvement in faith-based communities also contributed to their processes of desistance and personal transformation. This chapter includes the results of interviews with and observations of leaders of four faith-based organizations identified by the women as providing critical and ongoing support.

ASSUMPTIONS ABOUT THE ROLE OF FAITH-BASED ORGANIZATIONS AND REENTRY

Interest in the role of faith-based organizations in supporting and facilitating the successful reentry of the formerly incarcerated has mounted since the introduction of a federal agenda for faith-based initiatives. President George W. Bush through an executive order on January 29, 2001 established the White House Office of Faith-Based and Community Initiatives. The office was subsequently renamed the Office of Faith-Based and Neighborhood Partnerships by President Barack Obama, but maintained the charge to provide funding to faith-based organizations that seek to offer support services to meet the needs of individuals within their communities.

Underlying this charge are fundamental assumptions about the role of the prison versus that of the community in responding to the rehabilitative needs of persons with criminal histories. Prisons are places that primarily function to punish through social isolation. Although rehabilitative services occur within the prison setting, the demand for these services is often greater than the supply, which limits the participation to only select individuals. The lack of access to rehabilitative services while incarcerated for the majority of justice involved persons results in the State's overdependence on the discretion and capacities of the communities to which they return to provide needed support. The provision of education and job training programs and support services since the 1980s and the expansion of the prison industrial complex have increasingly become the domain of the social world outside of prison walls (McRoberts, 2002).

Another widely supported assumption is that faith-based organizations are "repositories of relational capital," (Boddie et al. 2010, p. 1) that can be mobilized to link persons with criminal histories to opportunities, services, and resources that enable them to become productive citizens. Studies indicate that churches help to mitigate criminogenic influences in inner-city neighborhoods by providing opportunities for fellowship and the delivery of social services (Jang & Johnson, 2001; Johnson, Larson, De Li, & Jang, 2000; Johnson, Jang, De Li, & Larson, 2000; Kamnick & Moore, 1997). Research has also found that faith-based programming can positively affect the post-release adjustment of the formerly incarcerated and reduce recidivism (Baier & Wright, 2001; Clear & Sumter, 2002; DiIulio, 2001; Johnson, 2004; Johnson, Jang, Larson, & De Li, 2001; Johnson, Larson, & Pitts, 1997; O'Connor & Perreyclear, 2002; Zimmer, 2004, 2005). A review of the National Crime Policy Survey, conducted in 2001 which included 1000 households across 50 states, showed that respondents believed faith-based programs were effective in reforming offenders indicating that public opinion also supports movement to engage faith-based organizations in meeting the needs of persons with criminal histories (Cullen et al. 2007).

Despite the evidence of overwhelming support for faith-based initiatives, opposition also exists. One criticism of the engagement of faith-based organizations in working with criminal histories is that most churches or religious congregations (e.g., synagogues and mosques) in or near high crime and disinvested neighborhoods are ill-equipped to undertake the delivery of social services and lack the scale, linkages, and resources necessary to address the complex and multiple issues affecting the sizable population in need of intervention (Chavis, 2001; Soskis, 2001; Wuthnow, 2004). Price (2000) in his critique of church-based outreach and social services programs, particularly among wealthy white congregations in lower-income communities, described these churches as exemplifying a patronizing disconnect between the "giver" and the "objects" of charity due to race and class differences (Price, 2000).

Well-intentioned persons that perceive themselves as members of a distinguished and privileged group of "givers" to the less fortunate may function to further ostracize and stigmatize those they seek to serve. The stigmatization happens by viewing the "objects" of charity as the "the least, the last, the lost, and the lonely" (Brown, 2002, p. 335), rather than as persons of worth who are deserving of joining the ranks of the "givers" who seek opportunities to be of service to others and make a difference in society. These criticisms call into question the involvement of faith-based organizations in the rehabilitation and reintegration processes for persons with criminal histories and serve as a reminder that not all faith-based organizations may be equally equipped to meet the diverse needs of the population.

COMMUNITY ASSETS: FAITH-BASED ORGANIZATIONS

Price's (2005) research as well as that of other critics implies that not all churches are the same and encourages investigation in the ways in which they may differ in their responses to the needs of persons with criminal histories who are seeking to change their lives. Faith-based organizations may differ in regard to their physical structure, membership, style of worship, auxiliary activities, and a host of other attributes all of which relate to their organizational mission. As assets within communities, McRoberts (2002) describes faith-based organizations and specifically churches as sources of: (1) empowerment, (2) safety, and (3) bonding among members. As a source of empowerment, the church functions as an advocate, agitator, organizer, capacity builder, and voice of the voiceless, underrepresented, and disenfranchised seeking to enable them to do for themselves what government is unable or unwilling to do; in this capacity the mission of the church is to encourage members to actively participate in programs and policy decisions that affect their own welfare. From this perspective, social and economic disinvestment, institutionalized discrimination, the lack of provision for a responsive social safety net, and other forms of structural violence are all the failures of the State, and as a result the community is a place where there are limited opportunities for residents to obtain a legitimate means to achieve the shared goals of society, such as self-sufficiency and ideally wealth. The mission of the church from this perspective is to respond to structural oppression by advocating for social justice and empowering the most vulnerable to demand a voice and active participation in policies and programs that affect their well-being.

The role of African American churches in the Civil Rights Movement exemplifies this notion of churches as a source of empowerment for vulnerable populations (Morris, 1986). As capacity builders, these churches functioned to create a web or community of mutual support and accountability by generating trusting relationships and social capital, that could be activated to effectively mobilize resources to build human capital such as job training, employment, housing, educational opportunities, counseling, and other services for individuals and while engaging them in organizing and advocacy activities in the campaign for social justice. Churches that build human capital and foster the development of relational (social) capital within the community in which they reside, and engage community members in advocating for change, not in spite of, but expressly due to, the social, economic, and spiritual challenges affecting the community's most vulnerable, including persons with criminal histories, function as sources of empowerment in their communities (Boddie, Franklin, & Trulear, 2010; McRoberts, 2002).

At times, churches in low-income areas may view the neighborhood where they are located as a host of failed social institutions (including those of the State and families) which contributes to a cycle of social disorder and moral decay that must be avoided.[4] To combat the looming threat of social disorganization and immorality in their communities, one response of the church is to function as a safe space, buffer, or bulwark against the threat of criminogenic influences that exist outside of the church walls. Rather than confronting the failures of the State, the mission of the church from this perspective is to addresses the weaknesses of the human spirit and to strengthen the resolve of individuals to resist falling prey to influences that may lead to crime and deviance. Church membership comes with an expectation that all things associated with life on the "street" should be avoided, lest one invite temptation and succumb to the seduction of crime and deviance (Anderson, 1990, 2002). Based on this perspective, through evangelism, the mission of the church is to be fishers of men and women by casting a proverbial *sacred safety net* throughout communities and prisons (McRoberts, 2002). As a source of safety, in fulfilling this aspect of their mission churches encourage justice-involved persons to commit to desist, obtain support in maintaining that commitment, and transform their lives by consistently resisting the temptation to fall back into life on the streets through active involvement in the church.

By viewing the community as the *evil other* (McRoberts, 2002) to be avoided when possible, some churches may risk further solidifying the divide between members (the churched) and nonmembers (the unchurched) who may be distinguished by race and class differences. Rather than evangelism within their communities, the mission of some churches may focus specifically on fellowship and bonding among a distinct group of members only. The needs of church members, and as a result their member serving activities including fellowship and denominational responsibilities such as evangelism in foreign countries or prisons, may transcend an emphasis on the needs of their immediate neighborhood (McRoberts, 2002). In this case, evangelism and recruitment within the community is less important than the provision of services to "those in need." From the community's perspective, this aspect of a church's mission may appear as symbolic attempts to "give" services without effectively welcoming and integrating the "objects of charity" into the church. The church, rather than seeking to create bridges between the "churched" and "unchurched," functions as a place for bonding and fellowship among members.

To some extent the social gap between the "churched" and the "unchurched" is a legacy of American tradition since churches have historically been segregated places of worship and fellowship that convene persons who tend to be linked by race, class and family ties (Putnam, 2001). Reverend Dr. Martin Luther King Junior's keen description of Sunday morning at 11:00 a.m. as "the most segregated hour" in America[5] speaks to the ability of churches to function as a source of bonding among members that are often linked by race and class and family ties. One might assume that race and class distinctions within the church might lead to challenges for faith-based initiatives that seek to effectively engage justice involved persons into their communities, yet with the high rates of incarceration and reentry affecting receiving communities in urban areas, the likelihood that members of churches in these neighborhoods may be related to or affiliated with persons returning to the community is strong, and therefore the potential exists for their engagement.

FAITH-BASED ORGANIZATIONS: EMPOWERMENT, SAFETY, & BELONGING

Of interest is the way in which the faith-based organizations identified by the women as helping to change their lives and desist from crime functioned as sources of empowerment, safety, and bonding. This typology of the missions of faith-based organizations is in no way meant to be an exhaustive classification. Rather than proposing that faith-based organization missions fall into one and only one of these classifications, this study suggests that these categories should be viewed as three characteristics of the missions of faith-based organizations that may vary in intensity and can individually or collectively describe different types of church responses to persons with criminal histories. To understand the ways in which these characteristics manifest within faith-based organizations, I conducted exploratory field observations and interviews with the leaders of the organizations recommended by the women in the study. Two of the leaders represented African American churches on Chicago's south side, one of the leaders was a minister at a Latino church on Chicago's far west side, and one was a leader of a housing and social service organization with locations across the city of Chicago.

I selected these faith-based organizations specifically because these were the ones that the women clearly stated were effective in facilitating their processes of desistance. These were the leaders who represented the organizations to which the women attributed their personal transformation. Of interest was how these leaders articulated their mission and purpose particularly in response to the needs of and challenges facing justice involved persons in their communities and the extent to which their messages sought to empower and provide a safe space and a sense of belonging to the women.

Case: A Safe Haven

"I knew if I didn't get to A Safe Haven, I'd be back on the street, and I just couldn't go back. I knew if I could just get there, I'd be alright. It literally saved my life." These are the words Bianca used to explain why she was relentless in her quest to be admitted as a resident in A Safe Haven after her release from prison. A Safe Haven is a Chicago-based affordable housing and supportive services agency. A senior staff member of A Safe Haven, for 20 years, refers to the organization as a "stabilization center," that provides addictions recovery services, housing, access to medical treatment, education and job training, employment and civic engagement opportunities to clients including the formerly incarcerated, homeless, and veterans. The organization's co-founders Neli Vazquez-Rowland and her husband Brian, both former corporate executives, invested their own resources to start the organization after Brian overcame his own struggles with addiction and witnessed first-hand the difficulties persons with less resources have to rebuild their lives.

The senior staff member stated that A Safe Haven's approach to providing a safe environment for residents is to focus on achieving sustainable outcomes with each client:

> What we do is make those outcomes repeatable, it is a systems approach that we have to addressing the individual, meeting them where they are at, connection the dots with employment health, housing opportunities, that is what is going to keep them healthy in a sustainable way—healthy. This is not a pilot. It is not an idea. It is a proven product that has been done thousands of times.

As the name of the organization implies, A Safe Haven effectively provided stable housing and a safe environment for Bianca to deal with her addiction and obtain job skills and related opportunities that contributed to her rehabilitation. According to the senior staff member, Bianca's story of multiple incarcerations related to drug addiction is not unusual:

> The story you heard from Bianca is what we hear repeatedly. With 5000 people served per year, many coming with similar circumstances. Bianca was arrested 122 times. We have a lot of stories like that. Her story defined who she was for 36 years. Even someone involved in that way can transform their lives. We help them identify the challenges that they are facing, how to overcome them, and connect the dots toward a new life that is sustainable.

For persons like Bianca, the organization provides them with a safe place to deal with their addiction and plan steps toward their reintegration. The senior staff member describes the organization's mission as focusing on identifying and addressing the source of the difficulties experienced by clients:

> The intention toward everybody that we see is to help identify what are the root causes of why they are in the program in the first place. Is it unemployment, drugs, homelessness, incarceration . . .? Is it chronic or the first time? That determines next steps and the development of individualized programs to address their specific needs.

A key aspect of the service provision and reintegration process at A Safe Haven is to identify what the senior staff member referred to as the "God given" talents (assets) of each client:

> Our intention is to connect the dots, get them back into society in sustainable way, and launch them on the path toward their God given potential. It's always about trying to find the gem that this person has, possesses, we help to polish it and help it shine. Whether it's the gift of music, public speaking, working with their hands, or technology, we help them. . . . We identify their gifts through observation primarily, but we also look at their work history, and take time to get to know them in a holistic way.

Although A Safe Haven does not formally identify itself as a faith-based organization, the organization has a nondenominational chapel and works with the faith-based community to provide services, support and opportunities to clients. The senior staff member observed that faith alone without the provision of comprehensive services is not enough to stabilize and enable residents to achieve self-sufficiency:

> I believe faith is a huge component, but faith without the other components is not pragmatic. We partner with faith based organizations to introduce residents to faith, but we try to tap into other existing resources [such as education, employment, substance abuse treatment, and mental health services] and what they have to offer too. We are not trying to be all things to all people, so we partner with others to provide comprehensive services. Together it is powerful.

The senior staff person noted that the commitment of employees to providing a safe environment for the residents at A Safe Haven emerges from their own trials including dealing with discrimination and hardship in their personal and professional lives. Using her own experience as an example, the senior staff member described why she remains committed to advocating for the most vulnerable through her work:

> I always had to prove myself. People get labeled and get thrown into a bucket because they come from a certain demographic, and you get stuck with this label and it is not true. Because of my experiences, I always fight for the underdog, and they prove me right most of the time.

A Safe Haven is unique not only in its provision of a sense of safety and stability to residents, but the organization also functions as a source of empowerment by promoting advocacy and outreach among its participants. One of the goals of the organization is to nurture clients toward increasing levels of self-sufficiency by providing opportunities for growth often within the same organization and others in the community. Approximately half of the 130 employees are former residents of A Safe Haven. Residents are also encouraged to use the skills they have gained at A Safe Haven to participate in civic activities outside of the organization according to the senior staff member:

> We give them tools that they can use to inspire others, and we encourage them to pay it forward and by making a difference. For us it is all about community engagement, including them in outreach activities, and encouraging them to become engaged in other community organizations and activities and for them to be a part of the solution. It is powerful when all pieces come together; our clients and the community, and with everyone working together, then we can create a robust model to improve incarceration, unemployment, and other risk factors highlighted by the media.

In addition to providing residents of A Safe Haven with the tools, support, and opportunities to improve their lives and their communities, Neli Vazquez-Rowland has been a vocal advocate for public and private investment in initiatives that view "housing as healthcare" and emphasize addiction treatment and prevention. According to Vazquez-Rowland, "There is a huge backend cost to not dealing with the problem up front . . . 80% of people in prison for non-violent crimes are there due to drug and alcohol issues. There is seven times more money spent (when someone goes to jail, than when they are in treatment)," (Barrett, 2012, n.p).

Prison may inadvertently be the last resort for persons in need of mental health and substance abuse services who have fallen through the cracks of a broken human service system. The ability of A Safe Haven to provide comprehensive services to the same and other vulnerable populations is intricately linked to their advocacy for systemic reform of the criminal justice system and other service systems that ineffectively address the root causes of crime. The senior staff person at A Safe Haven stated that:

> There is no reason for persons to become incarcerated to be able to receive mental health and substance abuse services. Something is wrong with the system. We accept it as the only option, but it is not the only option. There are things out there that work that can prevent persons from needing incarceration to obtain treatment, but unfortunately the response is often to start a new program and ignore what has been working for 20 years. What's needed is a total change in the mindset as to how services are provided to this population. Unfortunately, as Winston Churchill said, 'the government will eventually do the right thing after running out of other alternatives.'

THE CHURCHES

Of the women in this study, five noted the impact of churches in facilitating their change processes. The three churches identified as being instrumental in supporting their personal transformation were Vida Abundante in Cicero, a suburb near Chicago's west side, and two churches on Chicago's south side,

Ambassadors for Christ Church in the Auburn Gresham community and Liberation Christian Center in Englewood. The churches shared important similarities. Each church involved persons that had prior criminal histories and struggles with addiction in leadership positions. Each church also emphasized empowerment messages in their sermons and activities while providing a safe place for participants to engage in fellowship and receive motivation for contemplative reflection on their desired spiritual/behavioral change. Despite these similarities, the churches were quite unique in the way in which they carried out their missions related to providing a sense of empowerment, safety and belonging to their members and the wider-community.

Case: Ambassadors for Christ, We are all in Need of Redemption

The amalgamation of Ambassadors for Christ Churches in the United States and across the world that comprise their global ministry has the following as its corporate vision:

> To promote Godly Kingdom initiatives and programs throughout the world, that will alleviate poverty and provide guidance and structure for people from all walks of life to be able to realize their individual potential and live productive and fulfilling lives through the Christian Faith.[6]

Like A Safe Haven, the mission for the Ambassadors for Christ Church suggests that enabling individuals to achieve self-fulfillment requires strategic intervention to address both social structural and personal barriers, such as poverty and a lack of human capital respectively. While A Safe Haven accomplishes this mission through case management and the provision of stable housing, employment, and supportive services, the Ambassadors for Christ Church in Chicago's Auburn Gresham neighborhood realizes their mission through fellowship and providing a safe space for individuals to obtain guidance, direction, and friendly relationships to help them overcome barriers to a better life, as well as social services.

The Sunday church service is held in an upstairs room of an old former theater on the corner of 79th Street and Ashland Avenue, a noted hotspot for crime in the heart of the Auburn Gresham predominantly African American (98.9 percent)[7] community. Auburn Gresham covers just less than 4 square miles yet the population density is higher than that of the city of Chicago with 12,933 of the community's 48,743 residents per mile compared to the average of 11,844 per square mile of the 2,695,586 persons in the city. The per capita at $16,022 in Auburn Gresham is over $10,000 less than the city's average of $27,148. One out of every four households in the community are below the poverty level at 24.5 percent compared to an average of

18.7 percent in the city. Nearly one out of every four persons in the neigborhood is unemployed compared to one in ten throughout the city (24.2 percent and 11.1 percent respectively).[8]

In 2014, the crime rate in Auburn Gresham was ranked 6th out of the 77 Chicago neighborhoods.[9] Auburn Gresham is also one of the seven communities in Chicago to which high rates of the formerly incarcerated return upon their release from prison (Visher, 2005). One might be tempted to assume that the work of the Ambassadors for Christ Church in Auburn Gresham occurs despite the conditions outside the walls of the church, yet upon my visit to the church it became immediately apparent that the church's existence and work is an intentional response to the needs of the community.

Before entering the church "fellowship hall" in a corner room on the second floor of the former theater, the energetic effervescent sounds of congo drums, a piano, tambourines, and singing greeted me and drew me up the stairs and into an open door. My eyes immediately were drawn to a woman with her shoes off dancing up the middle isle that separated two sections of cushioned metal chairs lined in rows as pews. The seven persons that comprised the "praise team" played music, sang, and danced as others continued to enter the fellowship hall and take their seats. As the seats began to fill, one of the praise team members grabbed the microphone, raised one hand high, and chanted, "Jesus, we invite you into this place." Some of the approximately 20 African American children, 40 women, and a handful of casually dressed young men standing or sitting in the pews began to transition their clapping, singing, and dancing, into raised hands and began thanking Jesus. A member of the praise team sings, "Change my life Lord," while another one speaks in a slow impassioned voice, "Change what is in your life, everyone has something in their life they want to change."

The corporate mission of the church is to serve the needs of the poor, and this particular Ambassadors for Christ Church based upon its location in an old theater on a busy intersection in troubled community on Chicago's southside is aptly located to achieve the corporate objectives. As evidence that they are changing lives, during the Sunday service, a local senator entered and took a seat behind me. One of the members of the church later informed me that the senator's involvement in this church helped her to transform her life from one marked by poverty and drugs to become a public servant.

The inspiration to change was the theme of this Sunday service. Minister Perkins, a young African American man with a quiet strength in his demeanor presided over the service. Before beginning his sermon, he walked up the center isle greeting persons with these words, "The chains and yokes can be broken off your life in this worship service." His sermon was about "Biblical Stewardship." Drawing upon different passages from the Bible (Psalms 24:1

and Genesis 1:26) to define stewardship and make the point that people are stewards over all that belongs not to them, but to God:

> Our purpose, *The Great Commission that* was given us is to understand our role as a steward, here to advance the kingdom of God. God owns everything. Think about something you own, like your body, your car, your talents, or anything you think is yours. You don't own your body; you are only a manager of your body. The purpose of your car is the Great Commission. Your talent is not yours. . . . What happens when God wants to use you and you have ruined His body? Before you do something to your body, you have to check first with the owner. God may want to use you or his body in some way and here you are up until 2 a.m. and he wants you to pray for someone at 3 a.m. He gave it to you, why not let him use it. You are only the manager of all that God gave you.

Minister Perkins spoke with authority about the transformative power of God based upon the changes he has made in his own life. Before joining this church and becoming a minister under the direction of the founder, Bishop Joseph L. Sanders, Minister Perkins stated that he had also been "in the streets." At this Sunday service, during his sermon Minister Perkins made his way toward three young adult males sitting in scattered seats in the middle pews. Tattoos rose on the neck above the collar of the winter jacket worn by one of the young men, and another sat slumped to the side in his chair. Minister Perkins extended his hand out to the first young man and shook his hand. He then looked the young man in the eye, nodded to the others and said:

> Ephesians 5:15-16 talks about your time. Time is the most important thing you have because you can never get it back. What are you doing with God's time? Every moment of your life, you should be asking God what should I be doing with your time. Come with your talents, God can use you; come with your tattoos, God can use you. He is using me. He can use you. *[He repeats, "He can use you," to each of the young men and then turns to the rest of the congregation.]* In time, God will ask, what are you doing with the things I gave you to manage?

The music started again as Minister Perkins invited persons to come forward for special prayer and walked to some who remained at their seats to pray for them individually.

At the end of the service, Priscilla, who is a member of this church, introduced one of the young men to me as her son and stated, "I have been working hard with him to him keep off the streets, you know. . . ." Her voice fades as she looks at me for confirmation. I understand the pause to be in reference to the story she shared with me about her son who was murdered and her desire to prevent this son from facing a similar fate. I nod my head and say "yes" to affirm her sentiment. She tells me that her son has to hurry to leave because he just started a new job. She said this with such pride and enthusiasm that we all began to laugh.

Priscilla then introduced me to another young man that she calls her "other son." This young man who was assigned to her through CeaseFire for supervision by the Illinois Department of Corrections. Priscilla's CeaseFire program director is also a minister at the church, but he was not in attendance on this Sunday. The young man asked her for a bus pass and confirmed that the pass will be sufficient to last until his next meeting with her on the upcoming Wednesday at 9 a.m. As he leaves, Priscilla says, "I try to bring all of my sons to church with me. They need to hear the Word of God and know that God loves them. It doesn't work for some, but all I know is that this is what saved me."

The Ambassadors for Christ Church while providing a safe space for fellowship and encouragement within the church walls is also known to conduct outreach and prevent violence on the streets of the Auburn Gresham community particularly in the areas near the church. Renee who also is a member of this church described an incident where church members, intervened to deescalate a potentially violent situation:

> We were in church service and heard a lot of noise outside. So we went to look and saw a gang of kids in front of the door. We were in the middle of celebrating African American history month, and some of us were in costumes, Zulu Tribe dress and designs on our face. And we ran out there and said, 'No, not in front of the church!' The women in the church began to speak the Word of God on the corner right there in the street and telling them that the Black man is God's greatest creation. After about 15 minutes, one after another, they said, 'we leaving,' and got into their cars and left. The men in the church didn't say one word the whole time. Their presence was enough.

Renee says the church is known in the community as a "safe haven" where young men and women are free to come and meet to receive prayer and advice on managing difficult situations. She gave an example of one young man who came to the church after he witnessed an incident where he felt the police wrongfully mistreated his girlfriend. He and his friends had planned to retaliate against the officer. After receiving prayer, the young man agreed to refrain from harming the officer.

For the Ambassadors for Christ Church in Auburn Gresham the church is not only a safe space for cultivating the relationships, but the church also provides a sense of belonging to those who need to initiate and sustain behavioral change and a commitment to live a better life. Like Priscilla and Renee, some of the church members are also professionals who work with educational and social service agencies including the Department of Children and Family Services. These contacts within the church provide a natural source of support for persons in need of service referrals.

While Ambassadors for Christ Church achieves their mission by providing a safe space for fellowship and cultivating supportive relationships, the church also has affiliations with social service organizations in the community including CeaseFire and owns property in the neighborhood which provides access to affordable housing and opportunities for paid and volunteer employment experiences within the church and affiliated organizations. The breadth of support that is available at Ambassadors for Christ in Auburn Gresham and their demonstrated capacity to be a source of safety in the neighborhood enhance their ability to embrace persons, including those with criminal histories, and provide them with a sense of belonging within a community of care.

Case: Liberation Christian Center, An Empowerment Agenda

In contrast to the evangelical nature of the Ambassadors for Christ Church, the work of the Liberation Christian Center boldly presents an empowerment agenda. Bishop James Dukes is not ashamed to share that he began his journey of recovery from addiction and a life in the streets in 1995. Almost a decade later in 2003, he founded Liberation Christian Center in Englewood, a predominantly African American (98.4 percent) community on the city's south side. Although the population density of this bungalow community is less than the average for Chicago, almost half of the households are below the poverty level (42.2 percent). The per capita income in the community is $11,993, which is less than of the city's average of $27,148. Of the 30,654 residents in 3.07 square miles that comprise the community, one in five is unemployed (21.3 percent) and 28.4 percent have no high school diploma. In 2014, Englewood's crime rate ranked twelfth among the 77 communities in Chicago. Englewood is also one of the seven communities in Chicago with high rates of persons returning post-incarceration (Visher, 2005).

Liberation Christian Center is located in a two-story brick church building nestled among blocks of brick bungalows on the corner of 74th Street and Michigan Avenue. The traditional architecture of the building and neighboring homes are reminders of a community that in the past experienced less fear and more prosperity than in recent times. One might imagine how on Sunday mornings past men with starched shirts, suits and shined shoes once escorted elegantly dressed women wearing decorative hats as they ascended the steep staircase that leads into the sanctuary. Today women and children entered alone in most but not all cases, and the few young men tended to enter alone. At the beginning of this Sunday service, approximately 20 men, 70 women and 10 children were present and dispersed throughout the pews of the sanctuary. Most were in casual dress as they listened to the "praise team" begin the service with songs.

Bishop Dukes views the Liberation Christian Center not as a church, but as a movement. He describes Liberation Christian Center as the following:

> The catalyst between injustice and justice, hatred and love, separatism and compassion, poverty and prosperity, fear and faith, the have and the have nots, ailments and healing, the street and the sanctuary, bondage and freedom, ignorance and knowledge, oppression and liberation, sin and salvation, by destroying the man-made yokes of economic, political, social and religious constraints that prevent the spreading, teaching, and preaching of the gospel of the Holy Spirit.[10]

The mission of the Liberation Christian Center responds to what the Bishop identifies as a need to combat structural violence in the form of oppression, injustice, poverty, and inequality. This Sunday, wearing a long black cape over a dark suit Bishop Dukes entered the pulpit and drew inspiration from his memories of the Civil Rights Movement as he began his sermon on "Spiritual Warfare":

> You must be equipped to fight. Sometimes you got to swing on the devil. . . . You cannot be successful with achieving your goals without a strategy. Do you have a strategy? The Civil Rights movement had a strategy of nonviolence promoted by Martin Luther King. Many in the community were not sympathetic because they wanted to fight, but they didn't have a strategy. He asked us to go to meetings two times a week at the Institute for Non-Violence where the method of non-violence was taught as a strategy that was strongly progressive spiritually, and it presented a spiritual challenge to others.

Similar to Minister Perkins, Bishop Dukes' message offered encouragement and spoke directly to the potential of all members of the congregation to be of service, particularly those have criminal histories:

> God has the uncanny ability to use what is available but not what is expected. That's why He had to use you. Dust you off, pick you up and take you out of jail, bring you back home, and use you. There are many examples of how God uses what is available but not what is expected in the Bible. He used the Red Sea as a weapon to conquer pharaoh's army and he used Moses. . . . Spiritual warfare is the subject for today. Sometimes you get beat up because they don't know you are ready for a fight. Warfare is a fight for my spirit and stratos is strategy. The devil keeps beating you down because you are not using a strategy. Are you ready to walk into Battle or a parade? Are you a soldier? Be ready to snatch your grace, snatch what God has for you by the collar, and fight for it!

In the case that someone in the congregation did not have a strategy to successfully prepare for spiritual warfare, the Bishop offered this practical recommendation:

> Wake up at 4 a.m. and pray. At 4:30 walk through the house and say God is! At 9, take your Bible and read two scriptures, and say 'devil I'm getting ready for you,' and then read the 23rd Psalm. At Noon praise God for lunch, and at 6 walk through the house and tell everybody, "I love you, and we're going to make it." Give them a hug. Look at your children and say, "no weapon formed against you shall prosper, you shall live and not die." And then at 9 at night, worship Him and know that His Grace is sufficient. And then shout GRACE!

For Bishop Dukes, the church was less a refuge or haven *from the streets* as it was a mobilizer for action *in the streets*, and to survive *in the streets* one has to know how to fight. While the conditions beyond the church walls may teach persons to respond or fight using violence, Bishop Dukes sought to empower individuals to use nonviolence as a response to social, political, and economic challenges and hardship through spiritual warfare. Here the Bishop challenges those in the pews to be warriors that fight against life's challenges with resilience:

> Weapons, I got weapons – God has got this. He will help you to be ready to fight. God has brought you through so much. You are greater than the challenge before you. Become a general when there is a war. See how much fight you got in you. When you have no job, you have to catch the bus, you have to fight. What kind of warrior are you? What do you need to fight? Resilience. You know you have resilience when you reach a place where you become unstoppable. Paul is a good example of this, Paul didn't look the part, but after being persecuted, he said, "Nothing can separate me from the love of Christ" I'm a soldier. Every soldier has a weapon. Paul's weapon was his pen. Find your weapon. When I find my weapon I am armed and dangerous. Ask God to reveal your weapon, and say to God "Do for me what you did for Paul, so that I can use it to let the devil know who you are!"

Bishop Dukes stated that he is aware of the needs of persons in the congregation that have criminal histories and through the church intentionally reaches out to them to offer support. The church ministry supports a 12-step program to address the recovery needs of persons dealing with addiction and provides additional life skill and support services to facilitate the reentry process of formerly incarcerated persons who are returning to the community. According to Bishop Dukes:

> We deal with the post-incarceration traumas, reuniting with family, obtaining employment and staying clean to reduce recidivism. People are referred to us by

> word of mouth. We used to have a family reunification program funded by the Illinois Department of Human Services. We continue to offer youth programs in Chicago public schools and we have relationships with employers that has also enabled us to link youth to summer jobs and keep them off the streets.

Liberation Christian Center may function as a safe place of refuge and provide a sense of belonging for some, but clearly the intent of Bishop Dukes is to equip individuals in and outside of the church with not only services, but the personal tenacity to persevere in the face of interpersonal and structural challenges. His own experiences of being a civil rights activists to overcoming addiction and a criminal past provide inspiration to others and living testimony to the efficacy of an empowerment agenda in response to the needs of persons with a criminal past who desire to change their lives.

Case: Vida Abundante, A Community of Care

Whereas Bishop Dukes describes Liberation Christian Center as a movement instead of a church, the leadership of Vida Abundante describes this faith-based organization as a "Christian community" that was "born in the heart of God" and brought by God "to the suburb of Cicero."[11] Vida Abundante is not just a church or a community, it is an experience. From the location, the design, the fellowship, to the service, Vida Abundante is not your traditional church in any sense. Rather than a steepled building on a busy street corner or residential area, the open, sleek, techno design of the church seems aptly placed at the site of a former warehouse in an industrial district. The church is within walking distance of three schools and a growing business district in Cicero.

Cicero is located just south of Austin and west of North Lawndale two of Chicago's high crime communities. Austin was ranked the first among all 77 Chicago neighborhoods for crime in 2014 and North Lawndale ranked fifth. Both are high receiving communities for persons being released from prison. Both Austin and North Lawndale are predominately Black (86.2 percent and 92.3 percent respectively) with high rates of poverty and crime.[12] According to the 2010 Census, the population in Cicero is primarily Hispanic at 86.6 percent, and of the 83,891 residents, 3.8 percent are Black and 9.2 percent are White. Although the racial composition of Cicero is quite different than the nearby Austin and North Lawndale communities, the district is also characterized by higher than average rates of poverty and crime. The per capita income in Cicero is $14,741 and 19.8 percent of the population fell below the poverty level.[13] The crime rate in Cicero is 26 crimes per one thousand residents and the district has one of the highest rates of vehicle theft in the nation.[14] To respond to concerns about high rates of crime and violence in the area, CeaseFire Illinois operates sites in Austin, North Lawndale, and Cicero.

On the Sunday I visited Vida Abundante, Latino families and individuals representing multiple generations greeted each other with hugs and kisses upon entering the large vestibule. I was welcomed by a young female usher and invited to have some coffee in the church café before the service began. As they entered, several of the persons made their way toward the smell of the coffee coming from a room to the left of the foyer and others headed for the blue double doors on the opposite side leading into the sanctuary where the singing had already started. Instead of getting coffee I waited for Julisa to join me before going inside the sanctuary. Julisa is a member of the church. We opted to go to the morning service for Spanish speakers instead of the one for English speakers offered on Sunday afternoons. Julisa as a native Spanish speaker also served as my interpreter when needed.

The inside of the sanctuary looked more like concert hall than a traditional church, with a raised stage in front with large speakers, microphones, lights, and three screens facing bleachers along the back of the hall and several rows of metal-cushioned chairs on the main floor. The bleachers and seats in the hall were already filled with people, and Julisa and I quickly moved toward the few that remained open on the main floor.

The all-male praise team was on stage in jeans and long sleeved shirts energetically waving arms, singing, and dancing as the crowd followed along in similar style. The words to the songs projected onto the screens, but most in the congregation sang as if they knew the words by heart. As the music came to an end, one of the praise team members pulled out his cell phone and began reading the announcements which included information about the State of Illinois giving drivers licenses to persons without social security numbers. He also invited all persons to come back later the same day to view the *Son of God* movie at the church.

The same young man then invited two males and two females to come on stage for a competition. They were to eat whatever was put in front of them for a prize. First they put bread in each person's plate, then ice cream, then coffee, then ketchup, and finally topped the concoction with sardines. The competition then started. One man began eating what was before him, another man and woman tried and gave up, and the other woman simply refused, shaking her head as the crowd cheered them on. Moments later two more men dressed in white quarantine suites entered the stage carrying barrels with yellow tape labeled toxic and interrupted the competition by taking the plates and disposing of the food.

The Senior Pastor Andres Gallardo then joined those on stage carrying his laptop computer and asked if the audience understood the significance of the competition? He then opens his laptop computer and occasionally reading from it explained to the audience the theme for his sermon, "No manches el evangelio. No manches tu testimonio. The pastor continues to explain in Spanish:

> The bread looks good by itself, but then when you add all of the other things no one wants it anymore. So what's the meaning of this, "No manches el evangelio." Don't stain what is Holy; don't contaminate your personal testimony, your marriage, the Word of God. No manches tu testimonio, tu religion. . . . The bread may look good, but there is poison in it. What happens when you are hungry? People when they are hungry they will eat anything. Be careful, the greatest attack is against the Holiness of God.

Pastor Gallardo warns against several contaminants that if not avoided can tarnish an individual's ability to be used by God:

> God is very picky. Those who have committed to God must set themselves apart. They must let go of things that are contaminating your purity. Isn't God your everything? Then why not let go of that person. . . . Take a look at 2 Kings 4:38. Here in Gilgal and there was a famine. This place should have been full of God's blessings, because of its legacy, but they didn't apply what was their legacy. When they went to make some stew all they could find was a few herbs and a wild vine. The wild vine poisoned the pot. Elisha being a man of God said "Get some flour," and he put it in the pot to take out the poison. What was the wild vine, all the things that contaminate what is Holy. What is the flour? God, Jesus, the body of Christ is the flour that can save you. Ask God to remove from your life that which is contaminating it. The doors of the church are now open.

Unlike the Ambassadors for Christ Church or Liberation Christian Center, there was no specific mention or reference of redemption for or empowerment of persons with criminal histories during the sermon. The pastor's message conveyed that all persons are affected by contamination and in need of help that can be found within Vida Abundante. Five young men, seemingly in their 20s and 30s walked to the front of the church. The pastor prayed for them and announced that they all accepted Christ. Everyone clapped. More singing followed the sermon, and then the service was over.

After church Julisa introduced me to Pastor Gallardo and associate pastor, Reverend Ismael Vargas, who was also a former director of the CeaseFire site in Cicero. Reverend Ismael attributes his effectiveness as a CeaseFire site program director and in his ministry at Vida Abundante to his commitment to empowering "the young persons on the same streets" where he once engaged in criminal activity and dealt with addiction. When asked what is meant by the description of Vida Abundante as a community church, Reverend Ismael explained that the mission of the church is not only to be a safe space for fellowship and support, but to be a source of empowerment in and outside of the church:

> We don't want to be a church of religion, but a church that represents Christ. We accept those in need and help them to find there is a purpose in their lives. Over time we have reached a point both spiritually and socially to know how to impact community, as activists in the community. For example we are not only here on Sunday and Wednesday, but we help in the streets and deal with violence and other issues, such as struggling families. We provide counseling and act as a bridge between the church and the government. Because the community is with us, they come to our church, we can be their voice and share information about government and nonprofit benefits that can help the community.

Like the other faith-based organizations in this study, a part of Vida Abundante's ministry is to target persons who are currently and formerly engaged in life on the streets. According to Reverend Ismael:

> We have persons with criminal histories actively involved in this church. We believe the church is a hospital, a place for healing and change. We tell everyone God has a purpose in your life, and we believe that. We work with programs in the community regarding gang violence and drug addiction. They need to know that one's background will not hold them back. We have an open policy. We get their information on cards and start having a one-to-one connection with them to find out what is their need and especially to help them make changes in their lives. We also work with other churches, such as [one church] in Austin's African American community. We work together to address gang conflict and provide a safe haven for mediation.

To achieve their mission, Vida Abundante uses a systematic strategy to establish lasting bonds and relationships with persons involved in street activity. Reverend Ismael described the strategy as being grounded in community organizing techniques:

> We make them feel accepted first with a phone call. Then we schedule a meeting to visit with them and say how much we care and want to help them. When we meet with them our goal is to connect them to resources, women's groups, attorneys, or other social services, and then we follow up with them. Depending where they are, we will go visit them regularly to get them more involved.

Reverend Ismael stated that several members of the church are community activists, and that he has been an activist for 20 years working with Chicago Public Schools before becoming vice president of a parent advocacy organization. He described his work as, "my way of serving God. This is my life, I cannot separate that."

Community organizing strategies are also evident in other aspects of the church's outreach to different groups. The Connections group meets consist of a group of homes that are open at specific times during the week to those interested in fellowship. These meetings start with a discussion about some life topic and then connect the topic to a Bible scripture. Reverend Ismael noted:

> We have different connections groups, some for young adults others for singles, and another for single parents. We also have a marriage group that includes people that are thinking about marriage and others that may be struggling in marriage. Several couples, usually about 20 work with me and my wife and three other couples that are helpers for nine weeks. At the end of nine weeks, we try to help them to make the decision about what to do in their marriage, or plans to marry, and those who are still struggling we give them an opportunity to do it again.

Reverend Ismael described how he and his wife became involved in the church through the Connections group who helped them to strengthen their marriage and their commitment to God's work:

> After that we were never the same. Before, in my life I was involved with gangs. I grew up without a father figure and eventually got on drugs. I remember when the pastor saw me, he said, "we are going to pray and prepare you." He could see in me what I couldn't see in myself. Sometimes God has to allow you to go through some situations so that later in life you can use what you learned to help others.

He stated that his experience of personal transformation proved to be an ideal match for the kind of work that he is doing to help people change their lives:

> I remember being without a job and I had to make a decision. My focus was on looking for a job in a suit and tie, the kind of job I had for so many years, but that was not God's plan. God said, put on jeans and go into the street. So that's what I did. Then one day, [a local Senator] called and said he was going to open a center and said "I need you to apply. . . ." God was there and He took over, and I became the director of Ceasefire in Cicero. In that position, God was working to change the mentality of social workers, and the police about gangs and youth in the community. The police would ask why are the youth obeying me. All I could say is God was in the mix. . . . The youth would look at me and say, "that guy says God has transformed him and he wants me to feel the same." My credibility is God, it is not my past. They respect me, I am not perfect, but I am definitely not the same, and they see that.

Reverend Ismael remarked that his son is now the director of the CeaseFire site in Cicero, and that he finds it ironic that God would choose to use them both to intervene with other young men and women engaged in life on the streets:

> My son took over what I was doing at CeaseFire. My son has two bachelor's degrees, yet despite his level of education he has taken this path to use his education. He could have left the community and do something else, but he wants to use it to help the community.

The Vida Abundante experience is one that combines a sense of safety and protection from contaminants through support and a sense of belonging within the church with empowerment and advocacy throughout the church community. Together the church community provides persons with criminal histories with a unique opportunity to become engaged in a community of care. The Vida Abundante experience is one in which both native Spanish and English speakers of multiple generations and backgrounds may enter a physical space in a unique place to receive a warm welcome, sermon, encouragement, support, and invitations for further engagement. Persons with criminal histories may also benefit from the expansive reach of the church beyond its walls and into the community where they have built a network of supportive relationships and opportunities. Like A Safe Haven, Liberation Christian Center, and Ambassadors for Christ Church, Vida Abundante also provided women in this study with linkages to employment at CeaseFire Illinois.

COMMUNITY ASSETS & THE NEW SAFETY NET

Each faith-based organization in this study sought to achieve their missions in unique ways, yet they shared fundamental commonalities in their commitment to supporting persons with criminal histories. Each organization had persons who have overcome struggles with addiction and a criminal past in leadership positions and offered a safe place to heal, a sense of belonging in a community of care, and a source of empowerment. The experiences of women in this study highlight the significance of safe and supportive environments and empowering relationships as contributors to their ability to maintain their commitment to desist.

Chapter 3 discussed the traumatic experiences that preceded the women's involvement in criminal activity and subsequent decision to desist. The State through the criminal justice system rather than addressing the relationship between crime and the biological, psychological, and social consequences of trauma maintains a myopic focus on punishment which places responsibility for the treatment and rehabilitation on the community. Those released from prison may find themselves experiencing the same feelings of confinement on the streets of their neighborhoods that they experienced when they were incarcerated. Applications for housing, employment, education, credit and the basic assistance necessary to survive often require background checks, which contributes to feelings of being constantly exposed to the watchful eye of the State. The inability to obtain basic necessities because of a criminal history may result in a sense of helplessness and an acquiescence to a seemingly inescapable terminal sentence as an "outcast," whether one is in or out of prison.

In contrast to the streets and prison, some faith-based organizations are among the few community assets that provide environments that enable the persons with criminal histories to gain the support and resources needed to stabilize their lives. While the criminal justice system provides rehabilitative services that build human capital such as vocational, life skills, and job readiness training, rehabilitation alone is insufficient to address the complex needs of persons with criminal histories, particularly women. The findings from this study support those of other scholars who found that safe and nurturing environments characterized by mutual respect, empathy, and compassion contribute significantly to positive outcomes for justice involved women, particularly those who have experienced the trauma of emotional, physical, and sexual abuse (Bloom et al. 2005; Caputo, 2009; O'Brien, 2001; Richie, 2001). The building of social capital, trusting relationships, mentors/role models, and social ties helped the women in this study obtain access to basic resources such as safe housing, other supportive relationships, employment, and opportunities to become esteemed members of their communities.

Human capital and social capital are both essential factors influencing the effective integration of all individuals into mainstream society regardless of their background, but especially for those seeking behavioral change from a criminal past (Farrall, 2002, 2004; Brown & Ross, 2010). The organizations featured in this study provided the women with social capital in the form of trusting relationships, a practical doctrine for personal and social change and empowerment, and accessible examples of personal change and transformation among the leadership. These unique community assets also offered human capital through personal and career development opportunities and access to basic necessities including substance abuse recovery support, housing and employment. For persons seeking to change their criminal past, organizations like those featured in this chapter are the few community assets that stand poised as the safety net ready to catch them before they fall through the cracks of broken systems and relationships back into a life of addiction and crime.

LIQUIDITY AND THE NEW SAFETY NET

Bauman (2000) employs the metaphor of liquidity to describe a modern society characterized by the rise of fragmented social bonds and individualism. In liquid environments, freedom can be found through expanded choice, individualization, consumerism, and consumption. This notion of freedom erodes a sense of communitarianism and interdependence and delimits our capacity to be duty bearers for the common rights, interests and fates of the vulnerable and marginalized. Bauman contends that individualism feeds disinterest in politics and social justice, and breeds moral indifference (Bauman, 2000).

The marginalized are those on the fringe of a fragmented society. Those who dare can be identified by their extended reach seeking to grasp a solid thread among the frayed and weakened remnants of strong social bonds, while others may have succumbed to pressures to look inward to find something on which to connect their bootstraps. Perhaps those organizations that are willing to provide fellowship with, service to, and mobilization of those on the fringe are by default becoming the new safety net, the few solid threads of morality that remain woven into the eroding fabric of social justice.

This chapter presents evidence that some organizations remain ready and willing to provide a moral response to marginalized populations including persons with criminal histories. While their missions are admirable and absolutely necessary, their work does not absolve the responsibilities of the State to address the need for structural reforms that also engender social justice. Instead the missions of these organizations serve as moral reminders of the collective responsibility of the State and its citizenry to acknowledge the harms caused by the State that contribute to conditions that foster and perpetuate disadvantage, crime and violence, particularly in marginalized and disenfranchised communities.

Six of the ten women interviewed for this study identified their involvement in faith-based organizations as facilitating their commitment to desist. Of the others, two mentioned the support they received from their immediate and extended families, including housing, financial, and child-care assistance, another stated she relied on a friend, and the other reported that she relied solely on herself. In addition to these sources of support, all of the women stated that their CeaseFire colleagues and work within the community also strongly reinforced their commitment to desist. The next chapter discusses their work as violence interrupters and the way in which the work of peacemaking provided an avenue for the women to draw upon their own experiences and capacities to demonstrate stewardship while combatting crime and violence in their communities.

NOTES

1. See City of Chicago Reentry Initiatives, http://www.cityofchicago.org/city/en/depts/mayor/supp_info/ex-offender_re-entryinitiatives.html. http://articles.

chicagotribune.com/2005-09-15/news/0509150222_1_prisoner-re-entry-ex-offenders-illinois-department

2. See City of Chicago Reentry Initiatives, http://www.cityofchicago.org/city/en/depts/mayor/supp_info/ex-offender_re-entryinitiatives.html. http://articles.chicagotribune.com/2005-09-15/news/0509150222_1_prisoner-re-entry-ex-offenders-illinois-department

3. The seven high-return communities are Austin, North Lawndale, East Garfield Park, West Englewood, Humboldt Park, Roseland and Auburn Gresham as cited by Visher (2005).

4. Related theories on social disorganization originate in the early Chicago School of Urban Sociology. For a review, see Robert Bursik, "Social Disorganization and Theories of Crime," 1988. For a discussion of the response to moral decay in communities see James Q. Wilson and George L. Kelling, "Broken Windows: The Police and Neighborhood Safety," 1982.

5. Public speech on December 18, 1963 at Western Michigan University in Kalamazoo. See wmich.edu/sites/default/files/attachments/MLK.pdf

6. See http://www.ambassadorfc.com/#/vision-mission/4547603797

7. The source for the race figures is as follows: Jennifer Clary (2013). *Social IMPACT Research Center's analysis of the U.S. Census Bureau's 2000 Decennial Census and 2007–2011 5-year American Community Survey.* See www.ilpovertyreport.org/sites/default/files/uploads/Chicago_Neighborhood_Indicators_00-11_130109.pdf

8. Population figures are from the 2010 Census. See crime.chicagotribune.com.

9. Crime rankings by community are from the Chicago Police Department. See Chicago Police Department Crime Summary at gis.chicagopolice.org/CLEARMap_crime_sums/startPage.htm#

10. See http://liberationctr.com/home/about-liberation/

11. See http://www.vidaabu.com/

12. Austin is a fairly large community spanning 7.15 square miles and comprising 98,514 residents. Despite the physical size of the community the population density is higher than the city's average at 13,783 persons per square mile compared to 11,844 for the city. The per capita income is lower than the city average at $15,920 compared to $27,148 for the city, and the poverty level is relatively high at 27 percent. One in every five persons is unemployed (21 percent) and one in four have no high school diploma (25 percent). North Lawndale spans 3.21 square miles and houses 35,912 residents. Population density is slightly less than the average for the city (at 11,187 persons per square mile), yet the per capita income is $12,548, resulting in 38.6 percent of the community's households living below the poverty level. Of the population in North Lawndale 18.5 percent are unemployed and 30.4 percent have no high school diploma. Austin has near-equal representation of Whites (8.7 percent) and Hispanics (8.8 percent) as does North Lawndale (4.9 percent White and 5.4 percent Hispanic).

13. See U.S. Census Bureau at http://quickfacts.census.gov/qfd/states/17/1714351.html

14. See www.fbi.gov/stats-services/crimestats

Chapter 6

The Female "Offender" as Peacemaker

Violence interruption is a peacemaking process that involves identifying and preventing impending violence by providing alternatives for resolving disputes. Those that provide violence interruption services at CeaseFire Illinois are trained community-based professionals. For the females involved in violence interruption activities, their life experiences with harm, as "victims" and "offenders," function as assets when providing crime and violence prevention services with high-risk populations throughout the city of Chicago. This chapter summarizes the perspectives of CeaseFire Program Directors on the effectiveness of women as violence interrupters at their sites. The Program Directors that were interviewed represented twelve of the CeaseFire Illinois sites that reported they had female workers (a total of 19) who were actively engaged in providing violence interruption services.[1]

VIEWS OF THE "OFFENDER"

Literature on women in criminal justice tends to segment women's experiences into the distinct and implicitly exclusive categories as either victim, offender, or criminal justice professional (Muraskin, 2012; Belknap, 2007; Raffel Price & Sokoloff, 2004; Chesney-Lind, 1997; Belknap & Shelly, 1993; Adler, 1975; Hahn Rafter & Stanko, 1982). These distinctions overlook the observation that these roles often intersect at the same points at which race, class, and gender meet. The reality is that the female offender, victim, and professional may be more similar than different, as each possesses insight into their mutual realities at the various points at which their shared privileges and vulnerabilities meet. The lived experiences of the female offender, victim, and professional may also be embodied in a single individual, as is the case for the women in this study.

These distinctions are further reinforced by the response of the retributive criminal justice system which views the "offender" as a person to be punished for committing an illegal social harm against not only the victim, but the society at large. Punishment as a response of the criminal justice system, and by default the broader society, to the crime typically includes various forms of social isolation of the offender including incarceration, stigmatization, discrimination, and marginalization.[2] In contrast to the traditional criminal justice system, restorative justice strategies avoid labeling individuals as "offenders" and instead seek to provide the following responses to persons who have caused harm: (1) to enable them to accept responsibility for the crime, (2) to reintegrate them into their communities, (3) to ideally prevent reoffending (Gelsthorpe & Morris, 2000; Johnstone, 2002; Marshall, 1999).

Even without the use of pejorative labels, restorative justice programs risk treating persons who caused harm as offenders through the use of reintegrative shaming rituals. Umbreit (1995) describes reintegrative shaming as "a type of social control based upon informal community condemnation of wrongdoing, but with opportunities provided for reintegrating the wrongdoer into the community," (p. 32). The ultimate desired outcome of reintegrative shaming is the acceptance of responsibility for the crime, an expression of remorse, an apology, or an opportunity for reparations by the offender to the victim. Reintegrative shaming involves both the engagement of significant others (informal community) in the discussions between the victim and offender and giving offenders a "chance to redeem themselves" (Johnstone, 2002, p. 102). While the traditional criminal justice system through the courts and penal system isolates offenders from both the community and the victim which reinforces the likelihood that offenders may distance themselves from the offense, the aim of reintegrative shaming is to minimize the potential for offenders to neutralize the significance of the harm (Braithwaite, 2002).

Based upon the women's experiences in this study, while restorative justice is a humanitarian advancement when compared to the existing criminal justice system, there is a need to go beyond its prescribed avoidance of pejorative labels and use of apology and integration rituals by taking meaningful steps toward transformative justice. The women's experiences acknowledge the transformative potential inherent in confronting harm at the micro (interpersonal), mezzo (community) and macro (structural) levels of society through peace. Effective transformative justice strategies call on every member of society, including those with criminal histories, to take collective responsibility for and actively engage in processes to transform themselves, their communities, and the social structures of society as a means to reduce the perpetuation of individual and structural crime and violence (Morris, 2000; Pepinsky & Quinney, 1991; Sullivan & Tifft, 2000, 2010; Wozniak et al. 2008).

To view an "offender" as a potential peacemaker requires one to acknowledge the structural dimensions that contribute to the cycles of crime and violence in society while drawing upon the principles of transformative justice. The principles of transformative justice call for: (1) processes that are intentionally participatory and democratic, (2) values that are consistently supportive of healing, reconciliation and needs-based strategies, (3) ethical patterns of interaction that acknowledge the dignity and worth of every human being, and foster mutual respect and equity, and (4) opportunities that foster structural and cultural change (Braithwaite & Strang, 2001; Morris, 2000; Sullivan & Tifft, 2010; Wozniak et al. 2008). The offender as peacemaker perspective is aligned with the principles of peacemaking criminology which promote a sense of shared responsibility for the integrative processes that reduce the stigmatization and social isolation of individuals and groups that are labeled as "deviant" (Pepinsky & Quinney, 1991).

The offender as peacemaker perspective transitions the restorative justice context into one that has the potential to be transformative not only of individuals, but of ideologies and social structures. Table 6.1 provides a comparison of restorative and transformative justice processes and highlights the differing nuances in the aims, strategies and roles of the offender and community in each paradigm. Transformative justice processes that are derived from an offender as peacemaker perspective utilize community-driven prevention, conflict resolution, advocacy (mobilization), social care (community service) strategies to transform the ideologies that perpetuate crime and violence by engaging former offenders in critical roles as leaders, experts, service providers, and instigators of peace. The fundamental assumption of strategies that are derived from the offender as peacemaker perspective is that the needs and capacities of persons with criminal histories are not simply to face their obligations and obtain healing, but that they like others in society also possess the innate desire and capacity to demonstrate agency toward personal and social care, transformation, and redemption.

Women may be uniquely suited for community-based strategies that offer alternatives to traditional policing. Studies have shown that the strengths women bring to the work of corrections enhance both the policy development and implementation of community-based diversionary and reentry approaches (Cheeseman et al. 2001). Female criminal justice professionals, particularly in corrections, have been noted to be equally effective as their male counterparts, yet they may tend to bring a unique style to their work which has been attributed to their life experiences, skills and abilities as women (Britton, 1997; Lonsway et al. 2003; Lambert, 2007).

Greer (2008) suggests that women have a unique and acquired capacity to be effective correctional professionals because people from marginalized groups can develop special skills in that they must learn to recognize and

Table 6.1 Transformative Justice & Restorative Justice Comparison

Type of Justice	*Restorative*	*Transformative*
Aim	To enable them to accept responsibility for the crime, to divert cases from the criminal justice system, and to reintegrate them into their communities	To prevent reoffending (the perpetuation of harm) at micro-, mezzo-, and macro-levels of society through personal, structural and cultural change.
Strategies	Reintegrative Shaming, Victim Offender Mediation, Sentencing Conferences, and Peace/ Healing Circles	Community-driven Prevention and Engagement Programs, Conflict Resolution, Advocacy, Social Care, and Systems Reform
"Offender's" Role	Accept responsibility for social harm/violation and express remorse or apology.	Commit to desist from crime; Demonstrate agency to transform self, community, and society through stewardship or peacemaking
Community's Role	Provide a safe place for reintegrative shaming processes, and offer forgiveness and acceptance	Provide supportive relationships and linkages that overcome the structural barriers to basic health, housing, employment, and human services/opportunities. Offer reparatory and redemptive opportunities to persons with criminal histories where they can provide meaningful support to others.
State's Role	None	Cultivate a transformative context by reframing ideology, policy, programs, and interactions affecting persons with criminal histories Eliminate All Forms of Discrimination and Structural Violence

confront complexities in a number of contexts. This unique capacity heightens their ability to grapple with complex situations and understand multiple perspectives and vantage points including those of the dominant group (Greer, 2008). Prior incarceration and prior involvement with illicit activities may not only provide female violence interrupters with street credibility, these experiences may provide valuable and intimate insight into the factors that shape persons' decisions to engage in crime or violence. Formerly incarcerated women have been reported to be particularly effective at supporting and reinforcing positive attempts toward the successful reentry of others by offering information about their experiences with potential obstacles and deep understanding of the need for emotional support and material assistance (Muraskin, 2012). The themes of street credibility, unique interpersonal communication style, and a deeply empathetic approach to meeting the needs of others also emerged in the observations of program directors about the work of the female violence interrupters.

STREET CREDIBILITY

Another aspect of professional competence at CeaseFire is the possession of "street credibility." Violence interrupters are expected to come to the program having already acquired a level of "street credibility" necessary to be effective with high-risk populations. According to one female program director:

> We look for their experience with high risk individuals and they should come in already equipped to deal with this population. Violence interrupters have credibility because of their own experience living with other people in the streets. CeaseFire gives them the opportunity to use this credibility to uplift our community. (F08)

Another female program director notes the importance of having an authoritative personality and established relationships that can facilitate trust and cooperation among and between members of conflicting groups as the primary components that comprise street credibility for violence interrupters at her site:

> A good violence interrupter has to have an authoritative personality. They can't go into a conflict mediation with low sense of self or that will diminish their credibility. They need to have a relationship between persons and they may need different types of authority based upon the conflict, but the most important thing is that the relationship must be there first. (F10)

The "street credibility" acquired by females is as a key contributor to their equal effectiveness at diffusing conflict. Possessing street credibility not only functions as a means of influencing conflicting parties to seek alternative solutions to disputes, this attribute also contributes to a sense of fearlessness among female violence interrupters. One female program director describes the significant impact "street credibility" had on the effectiveness of a particular female violence interrupter:

> She was born and raised in the community, she knew gangs and had been around them all her life. She would always say, "I am not afraid," and she wasn't she was completely fearless. Walking around in a dark alley in the middle of the night to diffuse a situation was not a problem for her. (F07)

In this case, being fearless as a female violence interrupter was not attributed to mental prowess alone, but rather was earned through time and experiences gained "on the street." These experiences seemingly transformed what would appear to be dangerous situations to most persons into those that were perceived to be familiar and manageable by the women. In addition to street-credibility, the female violence interrupters were noted by program directors to possess related professional competencies including requisite skills, authority, trusting relationships, and level of fearlessness necessary to be equally effective as male violence interrupters in diffusing conflict.

Ceasefire Program Directors generally felt that females were as effective as male violence interrupters, particularly in their ability to control situations and facilitate trust and cooperation among conflicting groups. One male program director described the extent to which he recognized the equal competence of female violence interrupters:

> I look at the females like one of the guys, in a good way. We have equality in our office and in the program, women are equal to men. The fact that they exist in the office and program is a testimony of their equal skill set. (M04)

While all program directors acknowledged the equal competencies of the women, half of the program directors reported that some of the best violence interrupters were women because of the style of interpersonal communication that they bring to their work.

INTERPERSONAL COMMUNICATION SKILLS AND STYLE

Research on the professional competencies of women in criminal justice professions also describes their unique interpersonal communication skills and style as strengths that contributed to their ascension into leadership positions (Doll, 2007). The less confrontational interpersonal communication style of women has also been noted to contribute to a reduction in the level of violence in prisons (Boyd and Grants, 2005; Morton, 1991).

While CeaseFire program directors did not report that female violence interrupters had significantly better communication skills than their male counterparts, they acknowledged the communication styles of male and female violence interrupters differed. Women were described as more detail oriented, particularly in writing their case notes, and less confrontational than men. According to one female program director, the different communication styles of male and females were complementary and when combined provide the components of an ideal team approach to mediating conflict:

> Mediation should be a team approach. . . . It is good to have a male and female involved to mediate. Their communication styles are different, but not better than the other. In male and female communication strategies they can draw on each other's' strengths and assets. (F01)

According to prior research, the interpersonal communication style some women bring to their work in corrections has been described as a "calming effect" by their male colleagues as well as offenders (Morton, 1981; Crawley, 2004). This neutralizing influence of female officers on potentially confrontational or violent situations has also been described as a softer and more humane intervention style, (Cheeseman and Worley, 2006; Morris, 1987). The observation that some women may bring a "softer" more "nurturing" style to their work as criminal justice professionals should not be mistaken as a reinforcement of sexist beliefs about women as being physically and emotionally weaker than men. Sexist beliefs about women as criminal justice professionals include assumptions that female officers can put others at risk or that they should be limited to do only certain aspects of the job (Belknap 1991; Britton, 1997). The women at CeaseFire defy sexist stereotypes as they risk their lives to stop violence on the streets and intervene in conflict to save the lives of others.

Overall, there was a strong sense among the program directors that female violence interrupters exhibited a unique style that brought a sense of calm to potentially violent situations, yet this style did not diminish their contributions to maintaining the safety and protecting the well-being of others. Rather than heightening concerns about the safety, the presence of female violence interrupters seemed to have the opposite effect on the confidence program directors had in their capabilities.

All twelve of the program directors agreed with the statement that female violence interrupters were "calm and cool in tough situations." All twelve also disagreed with the statement that the presence of female violence interrupters "can endanger the safety and welfare of others." Program directors specifically stated that some females are more effective because they have a "softer touch" than male violence interrupters, particularly with male clients:

> Males are more comfortable sharing with female violence interrupters them males. They have to get more of a feel for the person before confiding in another male. Another male might have a motive, but they think the females (violence interrupters) just want to make a difference. (F08)
>
> In a conflict instead of seeing them [females] as potential rivals or competitors like they might a male violence interrupter, they see a female like someone like a mother or sister, and that alone can help prevent a situation from escalating. (M04)

Rather than referring to them by their first names, some of the female violence interrupters are respectfully given the title of "Mama" or "Sister" by program participants and other persons in their communities.

A male program director described how being female and the maternal qualities some associate with women were critical to the success of one female violence interrupter:

> One of my female violence interrupters is very good with males. Her effectiveness was because of her femaleness. Females bring a different type of passion. They are able to connect to males easier. It's like they have this mother instinct. Some females become a mother figure to the most violent persons in the community. I think it is because if a man says stop he (the client) will challenge him because he (the client) has to show that he is a man too, but if a woman says stop, he will calm down. (M06)

Some program directors, although agreeing that the style female violence interrupters exhibited contributed to their effectiveness, objected to the use of the term, "softer" to describe their approach to violence interruption:

> I wouldn't call it more a more softer or gentle side. Their style is more "nurturing," than soft, or I would say more "parental." (M02)
>
> They are nurturing, not soft, in that way they appeal to the more humane side of people. (F07)

This nurturing or parental type of style of female violence interrupters was identified as a fundamental need in their programs and communities. According to one male program director:

> They definitely add a lot to our site. Their sensitive approach to hostile situations and their engagement with victims and families is needed in our community. (M04)

Another male program director shared the observation that the nurturing style female violence interrupters bring to their work makes a significant contribution to the outcomes of program participants:

> Women have a nurturing effect. Guys have a heavier hand especially dealing with conflict. They (women) are able to keep up with their clients better. They seem more dedicated to keep up with clients. Women will go the extra mile to support their clients. Most clients they start with, about 90% come in without a diploma, and after working with them, most graduate with a diploma or GED. (M09)

The responsiveness of clients to the nurturing style or calming effect of female violence interrupters was not limited to their male clients. Half of the program directors reported they agreed with the statement that female violence interrupters were more effective at responding to incidents involving women. Program directors described female violence interrupters as having an innate ability to empathize with, "read" or interpret the details of a situation and formulate conclusions about the likelihood that a woman was involved in an escalating dispute in ways that seemed to escape their male colleagues. According to one male program director:

> Females are very helpful with identifying issues of a female nature that may be affecting the situation. (M04)

Other program directors, particularly female program directors also provided specific examples of the critical role female violence interrupters have played in their work with other female clients:

> They know how to manage situations involving women and don't get distracted like sometimes the men do. (F06)
>
> We need another female violence interrupter because a lot of the conflict starts with a female or a domestic conflict and female violence interrupters are very effective at resolving these situations before they spiral into something else. (F11)
>
> With the nature of conflict now, females are more involved, and we must have more female violence interrupters and outreach workers. Because of the nature of how conflict is changing and who is becoming gang members, we need more females. Women are becoming more central to conflict so we need more women as violence interrupters to do conflict mediation. (F10)

With increasing numbers of women being arrested for criminal behavior, the role of female violence interrupters reaching out to women and girls has become an essential component of the CeaseFire program.

Perhaps because of their ability to empathize with the experiences of other females, whether working in partnership with their male colleagues or independently to diffuse conflict, female violence interrupters were observed to make invaluable contributions to incidents involving other females. The empathy female violence interrupters use to manage situations involving women was also noted by other program directors as being a critical component of their programs. Here a program director describes an incident where a female violence interrupter intervened to successfully resolve a potentially violent situation:

> One conflict was started because of a woman and resulted in someone being a victim of a shooting because of Facebook. The conflict was domestic, between a male and a female, so we had both a male and a female do conflict mediation to prevent retaliation. Another incident was when a girl was going to two

different conflict groups. She was going back and forth instigating conflict. A female violence interrupter figured out that this was happening and did conflict mediation with the young lady to prevent conflict. (F10)

The significance of empathy in dealing with conflict is evident in the work of female violence interrupters. The following statement of a program director identifies the need for more persons with an understanding of dual subjugation based on gender and race (ethnicity) to facilitate outreach and conflict mediation activities:

> It is best to have males and females as violence interrupters. The gang demographic is male and female. Women are into stuff, and these young ladies can related to other women who have been through the same thing. We try to do gender-based outreach, but we need more staff. In the past we had more resources. Our community is 45% Hispanic and 45% African American. We only have one Hispanic female violence interrupter, it would be better to have at least one African American female as well. (M07)

PASSION

In addition to empathy and a nurturing interpersonal communication style, "passion" was also a term often used by program directors to describe the work of female violence interrupters. Passion was indicated by the women's demonstration of tolerance, flexibility, and commitment toward their work. Program directors reported that the passion the women displayed in their work affirmed to clients the messages that female violence interrupters will "meet them where they are" and "stick with them until the end." One program director noted that being open, flexible and passionate about working in the community is a prerequisite for employment at her CeaseFire site for female (and male) violence interrupters:

> She has to have an outgoing personality and a passion about the community. She has to be a good listener and don't dictate their opinion. They have to be open and flexible to the guys and their situations. (F11)

Another program director acknowledged that any concerns he had about what females could do because of their female status were eliminated when one of the female violence interrupters went into a men's bathroom to get one program participant who was attempting to be nonresponsive to the offer for services. The program director describes the passion and commitment displayed by this female violence interrupter in her work with her client:

> She had a passion for getting him connected to a job, and she was going to go the ninth mile to get him even if it meant going into the men's bathroom to convince him to that a he could live a better life. She gained his respect by going the extra mile. It's like when she did that he was thinking, "I must be important for you to go into a men's bathroom to get me," and that's all it took to get him engaged. (M05)

Another program director tells a story about how one female violence interrupter's passion and profound commitment affected an entire community:

> The biggest drug dealer or gang banger in the community—everybody was afraid of him—became our client, her client. He had numerous hits on him because he had did (killed) so many in the past. He grew up in the community and lived here all his life. She never gave up on him. She got him to leave the community and get his life back together. She went on to other things as well after that. At some point he came back to visit the community and he was killed. It was challenging because she had moved on with her life, but we had to get her to come back to work with us on diffusing the situation. She did come back to work with us after he was killed and she was able to diffuse any thoughts of retaliation after his killing.

Extraordinary is the person who after leaving CeaseFire for other employment would come back specifically to help de-escalate an impending violent situation.

Not all females have the level of passion, empathy and commitment to function as violence interrupters for more than a day. An evaluation of CeaseFire noted the program's high turnover rates (Skogan et al. 2009), which may be attributed to the high level of stress and danger associated with violence prevention. As one program director stated:

> Finding the right person to do this work is not easy. I have had others come in who only lasted one day. One saw a gun on someone she approached on the street and came back to the office and turned her jacket in and said I cannot do this anymore. (M06)

All but two of the program directors stated they never questioned or doubted whether females could handle the physical and emotional strains associated with violence interruption. The two program directors that reported they had some concerns stated that their doubts were not about the capacity of female violence interrupters to handle the stress and strain associated with their work, but that there were some situations where they were concerned for the women's safety. Here, one of the program directors describes how he handles these situations when they arise:

> There are some situations I do not feel comfortable sending women into, because of the more aggressive nature of some situations. One recent example was a gang situation involving all males where the possibility of gun violence was evident. I felt more comfortable not placing a woman in that situation because there were known to be guns. We ended up not sending anyone until it all cooled down, but later we sent a guy who was a former member of one of the sets. (M05)

The other program director who reported having some reservations was primarily concerned about the consequences of sending a woman into a potentially highly dangerous situation. Here he shares his reservations:

> One of the challenges is if things get physical. Some of the women can get in it and solve the conflict, but being able to get in to the mix to stop a violent conflict can be dangerous, and I would not recommend it for women. Males can come home with a black eye and that is macho, they get two beers for that, but "mommie" just gets a black eye, and if a woman goes home with a black eye, the husband says you have to quit your job, and then we lose a good employee. (M09)

One program director took a gender neutral approach to addressing his concerns about the safety by refusing to send anyone (male or female) into a highly volatile situation. The other program director took a gendered approach by considering the potential effect on the woman's family and subsequently her employment. Both responses may be reasoned, yet the gendered approach embodies traditional assumptions about the women's role in the domestic sphere and places limitations on their ability to equally demonstrate their commitment to their work. Although well intentioned, the gendered approach to dealing with safety concerns is sexist in nature. There also seems to be limited justification for the gendered approach since seven of the nineteen female violence interrupters were married, and fifteen had children, yet all but two program directors stated that female violence interrupters did not have more difficulty than males negotiating work and family demands.

RADICAL BRIDGE BUILDERS

The findings indicate the role of women as violence interrupters combines street credibility with the ability to be equally as effective as men in diffusing and de-escalating potential violence using a style that is distinctly calming, nurturing and impassioned while empathizing with and addressing the needs of their clients. Program directors at CeaseFire Illinois sites described female violence interrupters as being equally effective as men and displaying a softer and more humane interpersonal communication style that functions to have a calming and nurturing effect on persons involved in the intervention. This softer and more human style is in no way considered a limitation in the women's style of intervention, but rather is viewed as an asset.

The women as violence interrupters seemed to draw upon their unique vantage point as women representing multiple social locations within their families, communities and society to passionately empathize with the structural conditions and interpersonal situations confronting their clients. The female violence interrupters because of their female status and past experiences related to victimization and criminal behavior are uniquely equipped to meet the needs of others facing similar challenges. Their social location related to gender, race and class provides them with the ability to view complex situations from multiple vantage points and demonstrate profound empathy, compassion, strength and commitment to meet the needs of high risk and marginalized individuals. Similar to previous work on the concept of an intersectional approach to women's work in corrections (Belknap, 1991; Greer, 2008), this study found that an impassioned empathy coupled with their professional competencies and nurturing style enables female violence interrupters to be remarkably effective in confronting and diffusing complex situations to prevent urban violence.

The work of female violence interrupters was associated with a calming and nurturing effect, yet in most cases their roles and work are not limited by their gender. Rather than tokens or matrons as criminal justice professionals, female violence interrupters, working along with their male colleagues at CeaseFire Illinois, functioned as peacemakers that radically built bridges between individuals, within organizations, and across communities (Sudbury, 2003, p. 135).

Perhaps the women that are most committed to being violence interrupters are somehow a self-selected extraordinary group who have mastered the melding of multiple roles (in both the private or domestic and public domains), competencies (consisting of professionalism, street credibility and interpersonal communication skills) and social locations (including but not limited to gender, race, and ethnicity) into a cohesive understanding of self and others. This understanding of multiple vantage points appears to enable them to approach to their work the way most of us would like to approach ours, with limited inhibitions and fears, an acknowledgment of similarities and intersections, and a preeminent faith the promise of peace. This study on the roles of women as violence interrupters suggests that there is much to be learned in regard to our preconceived notions about the depths of human capacity for peace and its relationship to individual and community transformation.

NOTES

1. The nineteen female CeaseFire workers represent frontline employees with three different titles: violence interrupters, outreach workers, and supervisors. All three types of workers are involved in providing or supporting violence interruption services. The ten women who were interviewed for this study were selected from this group of nineteen female CeaseFire workers at twelve of the CeaseFire sites. For further demographic information about the nineteen female workers at the CeaseFire sites see the methodology section.

2. Rehabilitation programs that provide life and vocational skills, substance abuse treatment, and counseling services to offenders while available in the criminal justice system, given the high rates of incarceration are unable to meet the demand.

Chapter 7

Transformative Justice

Changing Patterns

How do we solve the problems we created with our current patterns of thought without changing our patterns of thought?[1] The traditional retributive criminal justice system as a primary approach to crime prevention and control has not only ignored options for victims to explore legitimate alternative forms of justice, opportunities for offenders to be active participants in initiatives to address the harm caused to individuals and communities have been undervalued, (Choi & Gilbert, 2010; Zehr, 1990). Changing patterns of thought about justice is necessary to solve the problems created by our current patterns of thought about justice.

Francis Bellamy, a Baptist minister and a leader within the National Education Association, wrote the *Pledge of Allegiance* in 1892. Bellamy helped to mold a sense of entitlement to the rights of full citizenship within the minds of children throughout most of the twentieth century. Now in the new millennium, time has revealed that contradictions and conundrums mire the ethos of citizenship. The women's and civil rights movements of the recent past have resulted in significant benefits for some, but not all, yet are not all equally deserving of liberty and justice?

The twenty-first-century citizenship conundrum makes the task of policy making all the more complex. The tenuous justifications for placing one or another person into the mutable categories of more or less deserving, without carefully taking into account the contemporary and historical impacts of structural issues and injustice, are becoming less tolerable. The state's response to crime, get-tough strategies, mass incarceration, and heavy-handed policing with impunity has become the impetus for collective calls for change. Incidents of social unrest are indicators of growing frustration and discontent with the status quo. Underlying the emerging twenty-first-century citizenship movement in America is a growing acknowledgment of the damage accrued by the contemporary and historical, anticipated and unanticipated consequences of retributive ideology affecting victims, offenders, communities, institutions, systems, and society.

The unrelenting punitive policy response to crime in American society is a result of retributive ideology. At its core, retributive ideology promotes the use of systems of power to protect those labeled as "the deserving" and to punish, marginalize, and isolate the "undeserving." Historically, this ideology has justified abuses such as slavery, genocide, segregation, discrimination, undereducation, ghettoization, deportation, racial profiling, police brutality, and mass incarceration. These atrocities are ill-fitted with the allegiance once pledged to a country that was to be "one nation, under God, indivisible, with liberty and justice for all." Seemingly as soon as the daily chants of children in the nation's public schools ceased to include the *Pledge of Allegiance*, organized protests against social injustice and in favor of equal rights began to wane, until now. On the nation's streets, from Brooklyn to Stockton, and Ferguson to Orlando, demands for an alternative to retibutive systems, policies, and practices ring and reawaken the American conscious to its allegiances.

THE CASE FOR AN ALTERNATIVE

The collective experiences of the women included in this study present a case for developing an alternative systemic response to the needs of persons in their quest to desist from crime and change their lives. If the recidivism rate is an acceptable measure of the effectiveness of the criminal justice system to deter criminal behavior, with over two-thirds of those been released from prison being rearrested within 3 years,[2] the system is failing. Given the disadvantaged conditions that tend to characterize communities receiving high rates of formerly incarcerated persons and the stigma of "criminal" that tends to limit their opportunities for employment, housing, social assistance, and other basic necessities, the question this study asks is not why do so many recidivate, but why don't more people recidivate.

Unfortunately, the answer to this question of why the recidivism rate is not higher, or what are the experiences of those who desist from crime, has little to do with the workings of the criminal justice system. While the women's experiences in this study may not represent those of all others who desist from crime, they provide compelling examples of what is possible. Their experiences suggest that for them the answer to why they did not reoffend lies in the combination of the use of their individual agency and the receipt of critical support from and meaningful engagement within their communities.

The transformative experiences the women described during their desistance and reconstruction processes are similar to what occurs during the preparation, action, maintenance and termination stages of the model for intentional behavioral change (Prochaska & DiClemente, 1983, 1997). The women's readiness to take action to change their behavior by obtaining necessary support corresponds with the preparation stage, while their growing confidence and ability to resist reengaging in undesired behaviors characterizes the maintenance stage. The termination stage marks the point at which they have zero temptation to engage in criminal activity, and their new ways of "doing identity" have become an automatic habit.

The women described their determination to find the community-based resources they needed to maintain their commitment to desist. They wove together a safety net for themselves, with little or no help from the State. These women represent the lucky ones, whose determination and persistence were met by opportunities to receive support, yet others with similar characteristics and tenacity are met with frustration. How much more successful might these women and others like them be if the State, in partnership with the private sector and civil society, was willing to invest in mainstreaming a systemic, yet community-based, response to persons seeking to desist from crime? Answering this question requires us to contemplate the relationship between individual agency, collective moral consciousness, and social policy.

John Fuller, in *Criminal Justice: A Peacemaking Perspective* (1998) describes philosopher Immanuel Kant's Categorical Imperative as a call to drive moral behavior and decision making by establishing principles and guidelines to create universal laws and solutions to social problems that are beneficial to all. In response to Kant's categorical imperative, Fuller drawing upon the work of other critics of mainstream criminology such as Hal Pepinsky and Richard Quinney (1991) developed a model for peacemaking criminology which includes the following elements: (1) the use of nonviolent and noncoercive means to achieve the desired ends by all concerned parties including the State, (2) socially just policies that are free of racism, sexism and other forms of discrimination, and (3) processes that are inclusive and insures there are no barriers to the full participation of community stakeholders, especially those harmed and those who caused the harm, (Fuller, 2003, pp. 86–88). Fuller calls for an extension of the model for peacemaking criminology throughout the criminal justice system so that the philosophies of nonviolence, social justice, community engagement and equal treatment of all under the law become standard practice.

Responding to the categorical imperative requires the development of a collective moral consciousness that views each person as possessing equal worth and being equally deserving of human rights, respect, and dignity. Ultimately the type of justice to be achieved by responding to the call would be transformative in nature not only by engaging nonviolent resolution to conflict through restorative justice practice, but also by seeking just solutions to crime by addressing inequality and social injustice through mutual social responsibility and stewardship. Responding to the categorical imperative involves modifying how individuals simultaneously allow themselves to define and be defined by the structures (social systems) that govern morality in society through the radical demonstration of care for others.

Changing the crime policy requires intentional change. Widening the policy lens from a myopic focus on retributive strategies as a means to "deter the pursuit of criminal-minded self-interest" is necessary to begin to see the potential of a shift toward a peace-centered and community-based approach to justice. This shift calls for the development of a commitment to a transformative notion of justice at the micro (individual), mezzo (community), and macro (structural) levels of society. This shift toward transformative justice is unlikely without addressing the gap in the criminological discourse on peacemaking criminology.

THE SHIFT TOWARD TRANSFORMATIVE JUSTICE

Transformative justice is a way of responding to harms caused by conflict, crime, or suffering by exploring and capitalizing on opportunities for healing and development presented by the harm (Morris, 1995; Quinney, 2000; Harris, 2004). Transformative justice is about using the energy supporting, conflict, crime, or suffering to create change at the micro-, mezzo-, and macro-levels of society by rebuilding individuals, relationships, communities and society through mutual stewardship, care, and concern with and for others. The women in this study demonstrated the potential of transformative justice in three ways. At the micro-level, to rebuild their own lives, the women used their individual agency to piece together resources including those within faith-based organizations, to weave their own safety net or web of support. Within their communities, they engaged in stewardship and peacemaking practice to uplift others through their work as violence interrupters. At the macrolevel of society, the women's examples of personal transformation and stewardship, *despite and because of* their criminal past, challenge popular perceptions, opinions, and ideologies about the appropriate response of the criminal justice system, communities and society to persons with histories involving drugs and crime.

The *triangle* or the Greek letter *Delta* is the scientific symbol for change and an ideal symbol for transformative justice. The apex of the triangle represents processes at the micro-level that involve behavioral changes, such as committing to desist. The micro-level processes also consist of the use of individual agency in the pursuit of basic needs including the innate need to demonstrate universal social concern or stewardship. Transformative justice and the ascension of the individual is dependent upon a strong foundation of mezzo- and macro-level factors.

Communities, social institutions and the way in which the relationships formed within them are the assets that provide a sense of empowerment, belonging, and safety. These community assets are the mezzo-level factors that enable transformative justice processes to be effective. *Empowerment* refers to the mobilization of human and social capital and the building of individual and community capacity for problem solving. *Belonging* is a sense of engagement individuals have within social institutions and their communities. *Safety* is the meeting of the basic needs including employment and housing as well as empathy, forgiveness, and redemptive or reparatory opportunities. Each element is needed to help facilitate change processes.

The macro-level factors involve the mainstreaming of ideology based on peacemaking criminological and transformative justice. This ideological change requires public and private sector and civil society resources and action supporting a commitment to: (1) reverse the effects of disinvestment, discrimination, and disenfranchisement on communities with high crime rates, (2) acknowledge the interdependence, dignity, and worth of every individual and community in society, and (3) zero tolerance for structurally explicit or implicit policies and practices that contribute to injustice or irresponsible and inhumane forms of "justice."

This model for transformative justice requires the acknowledgment of the interdependence between individuals, communities, and society. All three angles of the triangle shape and are shaped by the other. The implication of the interdependency of each aspect of the model is a policy framework which engenders an understanding that Change (intentionally with a capital "C" indicating a difference in degree) at the macro-level corresponds with change at the mezzo- and micro-levels, and likewise, Harm at the macro-level results in harm at the mezzo and micro-levels as well.[3]

The stories of the women in this study suggest that programs like CeaseFire that have provided former offenders with opportunities to meaningfully engage as peacemaking practitioners and stewards in and with the support of their communities not only offer opportunities for redemption, but also plant the ideological seeds for mainstreaming transformative justice in society. Rather than blaming social ills on either social structures that perpetuate inequality or on the lack of agency by individuals to pull themselves up by their "bootstraps," the model for transformative justice reconfigures the dichotomous "structure versus agency" argument. The model for transformative justice that emerges from the women's experiences acknowledges the interdependent "contributions of individual actions, social relations, and social systems to the process of desistance" and provides a "relational" view of behavioral and social change (Weaver, 2013, p. 72).

The relational view acknowledges the duality of human nature. An assumption of a transformative approach to justice is that the need to demonstrate stewardship, or universal social concern, is as natural as the pursuit of self-interests. This assumption may appear to be naïve, particularly when considering a response to a person who has caused harm. Whereas punishment has been assumed to deter the self-interested pursuit of crime, the relational view understands human nature to contain the capacity for both self-interestedness and compassion for others (Baruch Bush & Folger, 1994, p. 242). The women's stories point to the potential of compassion to create healing and to deter crime.

In *The Promise of Mediation: Responding to Conflict through Empowerment and Recognition* (Baruch Bush & Folger, 1994), the authors describe the relational worldview as valuing transformation, compassionate strength, and a balance between individualist and organic (tribal/communal) worldviews. The authors suggest that individuals, communities, and society have relational capacity, which they describe as the potential to integrate the strength of self-interestedness with the awareness of the needs of others (Baruch Bush & Folger, 1994, p. 243). Relational capacity is the transformative potential to maximize "compassionate strength." Compassionate strength is the agency individuals use to serve humanity (others/their communities), which requires and promotes a moral transformation of individuals, communities and society from a state of weakness or selfishness to what Carol Gilligan (1982, 1988) has called a "mature human morality," (Baruch Bush & Folger, pp. 232–233).

Based upon the experiences of the women in this study, mature human morality at the micro-level is indicated by their dedication to their work as stewards or peacemakers (violence interrupters) in their communities. At the mezzo-level, mature human morality encompasses the ways in which the community takes responsibility to act with care and concern toward all of its members (Harris, 2004), as well as provide opportunities for stewardship and acceptance. At the macro-level, mature human morality exemplifies the guiding standards, laws, and structures that promote "equality, particularly in the reduction of concentrated poverty and residential segregation; inclusion of all citizens, including offenders, in community life; mutuality or the promotion of incentives that make individual and collective interests congruent; and stewardship," (Clear & Karp, 1999 quoted in Harris, 2004, p. 123). Mutual human morality at each level of society is compatible with the principles of peacemaking criminology discussed by Fuller (1998).

Mature human morality understands *Self (an individual)* and *Other (society)* to be mirror images. As eloquently stated by Richard Quinney (2000), "Without peace within us and in our actions, there can be no peace in our results," (p. 189). Harris (2004) echoes Quinney's sentiments stating, "When we act for the good of others we promote our own well-being too," (p. 128). The relational view that underlies the shift toward transformative justice encourages every individual to find their place in processes to bring an end to harmful conditions, relations, and systems toward a more peaceful and just society.

Aligned with peacemaking criminology and a relational worldview, the core values of the model for transformative justice are nonviolence, ethics, equality, inclusion, empathy, compassion, empowerment, interdependence, and stewardship. Broken windows policing and other "get-tough" strategies when held up to these core values would be questioned in regard to their ability to create a more peaceful and just society. These core values when applied to restorative justice strategies may cause some practices to be questioned as well. Those restorative practices that place the responsibility of resolving crime and conflict on the communities most affected without an adequate and sustained investment of public and private resources are unjust. The burden of responding to the result of years of disinvestment, discrimination, and disenfranchisement which manifests as high crime and violence may be too large to place on these communities. Rather than "restoration" which connotes a return to a status that may have never existed, these communities need to be transformed; crime, when viewed as an *opportunity* to address its micro-, mezzo-, and macro-level causes, can lead to transformative change (Morris, 1995).

The stories of the women in this study are not intended to be a critique of the effectiveness of CeaseFire Illinois (Cure Violence). The women's experiences with personal change and their contributions to saving lives in their communities through their work are evidence of the need for programs like CeaseFire that give persons with criminal histories a chance to transform their lives and the lives of others. CeaseFire, although a highly regarded crime prevention initiative, is also controversial due to its engagement of persons with criminal histories. Even some of the most liberal advocates of criminal justice reform have difficulty wrapping their minds around the thought that "ex-cons" and "gang members" with felony and violent histories can be an asset to their communities.

Violence interrupters, as frontline CeaseFire workers combat crime and diffuse violence in their communities, yet doing their jobs often requires them to maintain ties to former affiliations, without engaging in criminal behavior and without working too closely with law enforcement. This reinforcement of "street credibility" by walking the fine line between being a distant arm of law enforcement and being closely acquainted with the criminal element is cause for concern among the program's critics. Any slip in behavior puts the program's integrity in jeopardy, and not all employees have successfully refrained from engaging in crime.

While police officers and civil servants often operate with impunity and fiscal support, CeaseFire workers operate under scrutiny and the ongoing threat disinvestment.[4] In 2013, Chicago Mayor Rahm Emanuel did not renew the CeaseFire's grant for $1 million. In March 2015, the newly elected Republican Illinois Governor, Bruce Rauner, in response to the state's $1.6 billion budget shortfall in 2015 and the projected $6.2 billion gap for 2016, has proposed a 60 percent reduction in CeaseFire's funding from $4.7 million in fiscal 2015 to just $1.9 million in fiscal 2016.[5] The sustainability of community-based assets like CeaseFire requires investment.

In addition to a lack of sustained investment in innovative programs, another problem affecting the shift toward transformative justice is a lack of collective efficacy or solidarity. Solidarity within communities is power, and power motivates action to solve problems. Communities that have solidarity acknowledge and utilize their power to decide what is a problem and how to solve the problem, and take a key role in implementing the solution (McKnight, 1995, p. 117). Problem-solving communities, "both prevent crimes and heal criminals," (McKnight, 1995, p. 139). CeaseFire is an example of a problem-solving organization that is specifically designed to prevent violent crime and heal both potential victims and offenders in communities that lack social cohesion. Of interest for future research is the way in which organizations like CeaseFire that engage persons with criminal histories, when joined with other community-based assets and private and public sector interests, function as mechanisms to foster solidarity and build the capacity of communities to solve problems.

TRANSFORMATIVE JUSTICE AND THE ROLE OF COMMUNITY

Responding to the call for moral reform of the criminal justice system involves a critical look at the role of community. Community can be narrowly defined as individuals living within specific geographical boundaries, but also in broad terms to include all persons affected by a harm(s). Based on the latter definition, community may include criminal justice professionals, community-based service providers, representatives of faith-based and education organizations in the community, as well as family members of the offender and victim. Chapter 1 introduced three views on crime and crime control (consensus, humanist, and conflict), and each view has distinct implications for role of community in the social response to crime.

The consensus view is associated with the retributive model of criminal justice. In this model, the State invokes social control through deterrence and punishment strategies involving policing, corrections, and the courts in response to the behaviors of persons that are labeled as "criminal." The consensus view suggests that there is general agreement in society on what constitutes criminal behavior. In this framework, the community shares the State's label of the criminal as being pathological and deserving of social isolation, stigmatization, and marginalization during and after incarceration. Communities also look to the State to enforce social protections against "criminals." Those that are released from prison return to communities that offer limited opportunities for support and engagement. Punishment for the "ex-offender" continues post-release, and in some cases they are condemned to life on the margins of their communities and mainstream society.

In contrast to the role of community in a retributive paradigm, communities from the humanist perspective are restorative in nature. The assumption underlying the humanist perspective is that ways of knowing and decision making are most efficacious when they are grounded in the values of compassion, cooperation, collective responsibility and intolerance for injustice (Zehr, 2002). Restorative justice strategies engage the community in the condemnation of wrongdoing and the provision of opportunities for reintegrating the wrongdoer into the community (Braithwaite, 2002; Umbreit, 1995, p. 32). Members of the community actively engage in processes to resolve conflict and elicit apologies for the harm caused. While restorative justice processes are known to be effective at diverting cases from the criminal justice system, additional processes may be required to facilitate reintegration and deal with the complex individual, interpersonal, and structural issues that influence crime and reoffending (Crawford & Newburn, 2003; Dyck, 2000). Transformative justice strategies address the limitations of restorative justice by intentionally engaging the community in activities to facilitate the desistance from crime while mobilizing assets and resources to address the structural harms that contribute to crime.

The conflict view on crime prevention and control is aligned with the transformative justice paradigm. The role of the community from the conflict view is to facilitate processes for reconstruction from the micro- to macro-levels of society. By engaging in practices that are aligned with universal social concern, stewardship and peacemaking, the community functions as a capacity builder of human and social capital, a source of advocacy and empowerment against social injustice, and a provider of a sense of safety, basic needs, and meaningful opportunities for persons with criminal histories to contribute to the well-being of others and improve their communities. These types of practices go beyond the healing of and mediation between offenders and victims to empowering them to work as agents of change.

As change agents, individuals become conscious or aware of the constraining and enabling factors, both personal and structural. During the reconstruction process, individuals also reflect on the ways they have given up their personal power in the past by rendering a circumscribed, oppressed, and *subjective reality as absolute* (Bernard, 2013, Jackson, 2001). The women in this study, during their reconstruction processes, actively engaged in the difficult "emotion work" (Reger, 2004; Hochschild, 1979) required to confront contradictions within themselves and their environments that kept them bound to a life of crime. This process of challenging internal constructions of self in response to hegemonic ideologies can be equated to the loss of a false consciousness and an increased awareness or consciousness-raising toward the possibility of an alternative reality (Bart, 1982; Fanon, 1963). The work of the women as peacemakers enabled them to continually challenge hegemonic ideologies about their worth and potential despite their criminal histories. In their process of reconstruction, they each demonstrated a willingness to ask themselves the critical question, *to what extent is the oppressor I?*

Each of the women responded by reinforcing their commitment to desist from crime and seeking support and opportunities to become stewards in their communities. The support they received included engaging them in opportunities to transform their communities. By being actively and meaningfully engaged in opportunities to demonstrate stewardship in troubled communities, the women's work as peacemakers enabled them to break free from oppressive ideologies about the worth and potential of persons with criminal histories.

Transformative justice strategies strengthen restorative justice practices by adding the principles of stewardship, the mobilization of community assets and resources to solve problems, and the mainstreaming of peacemaking ideology. Restorative justice values opportunities for healing personal and interpersonal suffering by enabling "offenders" to accept responsibility for the harm caused, address their obligations to the victim, and receive support toward reintegration. Transformative justice includes these values, but ultimately would include strategies to heal the suffering caused by structural factors such as discrimination, inequality, and disinvestment that contribute to cycles of crime and violence in society. Restorative practices become transformative in nature when they view and create opportunities to view the "offender" as *peacemaker* and valued contributor to community and society.

As leaders, experts, service providers, and change agents, persons with criminal histories hold the potential to help communities challenge retributive ideologies that promote get-tough strategies as the primary means to deter crime. In a transformative paradigm, persons with criminal histories function as "wounded healers" (Maruna, 2001; Nouwen, 1972), by engaging in opportunities to use their past experiences as the impetus for change and by becoming role models or stewards in their communities. The women in this study can be considered reformers, whose work in their communities as peacemakers contradicts popular images that shape our understanding of persons with criminal histories. Their experiences give voice to critics of the existing criminal justice system, who point to the conditions that contribute to its revolving door and the corresponding recidivism rate, and collectively proclaim, "THERE MUST BE AN ALTERNATIVE." Transformative justice promotes alternatives to a one-size-fits all criminal justice system.

RESISTANCE TO CHANGE

Transformative justice grounds key elements of restorative justice, peacemaking criminology, feminist criminology, and community-based practice into a relational worldview. The fundamental link between each element is the notion of interdependence. Acknowledging the potential of collective resources and assets requires accepting that *no one is expendable.*

Confrontation, agitation, and resistance to the notion of interdependence is a predicted response, particularly by vested interests who benefit from the status quo and by individuals simply not willing to adapt to the tide of a new era. The ideological battle of views on crime and crime control in America involves our most fundamental notions of self, the State, and our responsibilities to one another in society. Challenging these fundamental ideals in ourselves and others may cause some discomfort, denial, and discord. Vehement resistance may also come from those who consider themselves to have liberal tendencies yet enjoy the comforts afforded by distancing themselves from the lives of those labeled as "undeserving." Resistance to change is natural and perhaps needed to spark awareness, encourage reflection, and radically loosen the roots that bind our future to an oppressive system of justice.

Another threat to transformative justice is symbolic change. Substantive change in social policy responses to crime that support a retributive practices is unlikely without a shift in the way the social, political, and economic systems reinforce class and power differences. Liberal sounding legislation such as deinstitutionalization or early release for nonviolent offenders, ending mandatory sentencing, and relaxing marijuana legislation could function to disproportionately benefit those with power. Decriminalizing marijuana would benefit those who have the power and money to "invest" in marijuana enterprises, while others with less power would be relegated to "consumer" status. The socioeconomic disparity between the communities of the "investors" and those of the "consumers" would continue to widen with blame for the inequality gap placed on the "consumers" for their inability to work hard, save, and invest. Consequently, social and economic inequality when coupled with disinvestment in the poorest communities further solidifies the social location of the most vulnerable on the margins of society.

Advocacy for prison abolition fits within the transformative justice paradigm (Morris, 1995), yet the return of the formerly incarcerated to underserved, disenfranchised, and disadvantaged communities without an integrated system of sufficient support is also inhumane. Each community that is receiving high numbers of the formerly incarcerated needs to have access to a seamless system of dedicated resources established for the specific purpose of linking every returning citizen to employment, housing, education/training, family reunification, substance abuse recovery, mental health, and other social support as well as connects them to opportunities for stewardship, social capital building, community engagement and empowerment. Increasing access to this type of system requires strategic investment. Convenient knee-jerk solutions to the state and federal budget crisis without adequate resources to support receiving communities may serve to reinforce or worse exacerbate the same conditions they seek to remedy.

Currently in Illinois, multiple organizations and collaborations have as their mandate or mission to provide linkages to services to divert persons from entering the criminal justice system or to reduce recidivism among returning citizens. Networking among the organizations may occur, yet the integration of these services into a seamless system of care that addresses the gaps in services, and tracks the processes, progress, and outcomes for every returnee to communities does not exist. Rather than a seamless system, those seeking to desist from crime are met with an array of duplicative and fragmented services that often fail to adequately address their immediate needs for accessing safe and affordable housing, finding gainful employment, recovery support, and reuniting with children and family. An important point for policymakers and practitioners to keep in mind when planning and coordinating services is the extremely high levels of unmet immediate needs of persons returning to the community.

The array of fragmented and duplicated services gives the impression of service availability, yet access to employment and housing providers to this population are limited. The gap in the need or demand versus the supply for employment and housing services compounds the sense of frustration and hopelessness felt by some returning citizens that may lead to reoffending. With returning citizens receiving so few services, compared to what they need, there is little wonder why they recidivate (Malik-Kane & Visher, 2008). Persons returning to communities with fragmented and duplicated services and limited access to employment, housing, and opportunities to build social and human capital are likely to reoffend.

Treatment Alternatives for Safe Communities (TASC) is an innovative example of a practical approach to transformative justice. TASC is a nonprofit organization that is funded by the State of Illinois to provide case management services to persons with criminal histories overcome drug problems and other health conditions. TASC serves as a lead agency or broker for diversionary (probation) and reentry (parole) services for youth and adults involved in substance abuse-related crimes. With 50 sites across the state of Illinois, TASC also operates within the Sheridan Correctional Center and Southwestern Illinois Correctional Center, which are the only facilities of their kind in Illinois designed as a therapeutic prison drug treatment and community reentry programs for persons with substance abuse-related arrests. In addition to engaging inmates in a rigorous curriculum and substance abuse treatment within the prison, TASC personnel begin to make assessments and service connections to prepare inmates for reentry 120 days before their release.

One of the key components of the release process is the integrated case staffing that occurs the month before the inmate is discharged. Present at the staffing with each inmate are representatives of TASC, Parole, and other community-based service providers that are available to assist with the inmate's transition. During the staffing, the release date and expected housing arrangements are confirmed with the inmate. The inmate also learns of the expectations for them to check in with TASC and their parole agent immediately upon their arrival at their designated address. The program participants must also complete a minimum of 25 hours of treatment and be available to meet at designated times with their TASC case manager and parole agent. TASC case managers are committed to following up with clients a minimum of six months after their release and are available for support throughout their parole. In the past, TASC has hired persons with criminal histories to provide support to returning citizens.

During the case staffing, service representatives discuss the inmate's employment, education, substance and mental health treatment needs and plans. Through TASC, inmates without solid employment are referred to temporary agencies, and those without stable housing are linked to transitional housing facilities. Inmates who desire to obtain their GED and those with mental health, anger management, and substance abuse treatment or recovery support needs are referred to providers in or near the communities where they will reside upon their release. Those that obtain their GED are offered a 90-day reduction from their parole. Those that successfully complete TASC, drug treatment, and aftercare services through the prison drug treatment and community reentry programs have a 44 percent lower likelihood of return to prison within 7 years.[6]

Funding for the prerelease and reentry services provided by TASC comes from the Illinois Department of Corrections (IDOC), the Illinois Department of Human Services Division of Alcoholism and Substance Abuse (DASA).

Despite their effectiveness, funding for TASC, like other human services has been affected by the State's budgetary constraints. The State's focus on fiscal austerity has taken precedence over the fiscal astuteness of supporting programs like TASC. Every dollar dedicated to programs like TASC is likely to produce savings in other areas by the State. Programs like TASC, by helping to prevent reoffending reduces the burden on other State expenditures including the criminal justice, public health, and homeless service systems. Understanding the value and social benefits of programs like TASC is dependent upon the development of compassionate strength among policy makers.

Perhaps lessons could be learned from the social response to homelessness. Compassion as a response to the homeless is rooted in American history. Veterans, widows and orphans affected by war, families who lost everything in the Great Depression, and immigrants in need of settlement houses were met with sympathetic support by American public and philanthropic interests. Faith-based and other public and private sector organizations continue to readily provide assistance, such as volunteer manpower and financial support to feed, clothe, and house homeless adults and children, without asking who among them are the "deserving" or "undeserving." Thoughts about the past behaviors or current conditions of those in need are muted by compassionate strength and the humanitarian desire to give to "the homeless"—a label that seems more socially acceptable than "ex-offender" or "former gangbanger." How much of the success of the one-third of the formerly incarcerated that do not recidivate within 3 years is due to the existence of the homeless services system and the willingness of the public to *give* to "the homeless" is a topic worthy of further study.

The goal of addressing the needs of persons returning to their communities and others seeking to desist from crime aligns with that of homelessness prevention. Without a systemic response to the specific needs for housing, employment, and supportive services for persons returning to communities, "many shelters have become de facto drop-off centers for ex-offenders," (Martin, 2015, n.p.). This reality in some cases may contribute to safety concerns, particularly for those shelter providers that are ill equipped to deal with the multiple needs of the formerly incarcerated. The homeless service system may be the de facto point of reentry for large numbers of the formerly incarcerated who lack family, friends or other ties to stable housing.

A Safe Haven is another example of a program that fits within the transformative justice paradigm. The Illinois Department of Corrections works with transitional housing organizations like A Safe Haven to link returning citizens to comprehensive services including linkages to job training and placement, permanent housing, and substance abuse recovery services. At A Safe Haven, the formerly incarcerated also obtain opportunities to engage in community service and stewardship activities that enable them to obtain the human and social capital needed to maintain their stability after leaving the program. Organizations like A Safe Haven that have the capacity and vision to provide comprehensive services to persons with criminal histories are rare, and to meet the demand for these types of programs funding is critical.

Linking federal, state, and local funding for reentry and homeless services may be one way to address the need for a comprehensive reentry (desistance) system. Finding innovative ways to integrate and expand services and provide incentives to foster the engagement of community-based civil society (including faith-based organizations) and the private sector to address the diverse needs of persons seeking to desist from crime, particularly returning citizens would represent significant steps toward transforming the social response to persons with criminal histories.

Opponents of a more humane response to persons with a criminal history may suggest that investing in programs for "criminals" contributes to the motto, "crime pays" by seemingly rewarding persons for having a criminal history. The underlying assumption is that these persons, due to their crime and despite being released after completing their sentences, have no right to employment, housing, education, and other basic necessities including the right to be an engaged, accepted, and valued member of a community. Upholding the belief that persons with criminal histories are "undeserving" or "expendable" is contrary to the notions of interdependency and collective responsibility which are at the core of the model for transformative justice. The time has come to acknowledge our interdependency and collective responsibility to respond to the structures and conditions that contribute to crime and injustice by advocating for the development of systems and communities that support and engage those seeking to desist from crime as a remedy to recidivism.

A TIME OF TRANSFORMATION

According to Angela Davis, Political activist and distinguished professor emerita of History of Consciousness and Feminist Studies at the University of California, Santa Cruz, "We are in a time of transformation. There is such potential for change. All over this country from Ferguson to New York City to Washington—indeed, in other parts of the world. . . ."[7] I agree. The time is ripe for forwarding ideas about the change we want to see in the criminal justice system. Policies and interventions that promote the creation and sustainability of communities of care, rebuild neighborhoods, and encourage social responsibility, stewardship and community cohesion hold the potential to provide an alternative. This type of change would require public and private sector partnerships with the support of faith-based organizations and civil society to encourage and model examples of social responsibility that uphold the principles of transformative justice.

Organizations like CeaseFire when joined with other community-based resources and private and public sector interests could become a mechanism building the capacity of communities to promote transformative justice. Faith-based organizations working in collaboration with alternative organizations that provide peacemaking opportunities hold the potential to support of the principles of transformative justice, by teaching, demonstrating, and providing opportunities for stewardship, engagement, and empowerment for persons with criminal histories.

An unexpected finding in this study was the importance of the role of the women in this study as *othermothers.* As they fulfilled fulfilling their responsibilities to provide violence interruption services in communities throughout Chicago, the young persons the women encountered viewed and accepted them as othermothers. The women seemed to fill a void for some young persons whose relationships with their own parents were strained or nonexistent. Their acceptance as othermothers points to the potential of developing informal kinship networks that could intervene and support young people that are returning to the community or being diverted from the system. Similar to mentoring programs, such as *Big Brothers, Big Sisters,* kinship networks would provide young persons with role models, except these mentors would be persons like those at CeaseFire who have the street credibility and paraprofessional training in conflict resolution, violence interruption, making service, housing, and employment linkages, and other requisite skills to provide critical support and encourage a commitment to desist from crime.

Change happens when strength of individual agency combines with compassion to transform conditions, relationships, and structures. Faith-based organizations have historically been the places where compassionate strength has been collectively galvanized, organized, and mobilized to advocate for change from the micro- to the macro-levels of society. In the twenty-first century, they continue to represent social centers in communities where inspirational messages based on the principles of transformative justice can be regularly shared and activated within and beyond the pews. To become *a safe haven* for persons with criminal histories and to challenge ideology, laws, and practices that perpetuate social injustice, faith-based organizations may benefit from support in the form of community organizers, advocacy and sensitivity training, and program development to build their capacity to actively engage in transformative justice practices. Although faith-based organizations remain an accepted hub for mobilizing public and private sector support for vulnerable populations locally and across the globe, they are not the only places where compassionate strength can be developed and mobilized.

It is within the church walls, on the streets, in the schools, boardrooms, living rooms, court rooms, and in all spaces where human interaction occurs that the collective culpability of all members of society in perpetuating oppressive ideologies must be regularly questioned as a matter of introspective contemplation and consciousness-raising. Within each of those sacred spaces lies the transformative potential of the answer to the question, what are we willing to do to move toward an increasingly good and just society. The vein of our evolution toward the guiding scales of justice rests in our response to those who have criminal histories and others with restricted means to escape the margins.

STATUS UPDATE

For the women in this study who remain at CeaseFire, the way forward is clear. As of February 2015, just prior to the announcement of proposed State budget cuts that threaten CeaseFire's funding, all but three of the women continued to work for the organization. Of the three who no longer work for the organization, Julisa moved with her family to a suburb of Chicago, found other employment closer to home, and intends to pursue her Bachelor's degree in psychology. She misses her work at CeaseFire, and has started a blog designed to motivate young people to become engaged in their communities, improve their relationships and end violence. The two women who began working at CeaseFire as a part of a job training program, Bobbi and Gina, left after completing their program requirements. As of February 2015, neither Bobbi nor Gina had reoffended.

The seven women who remained at CeaseFire as of February 2015 continued to thrive. Bianca proudly reported that she was actively engaged in the lives of her five children, and her four grandchildren call her "Grandma." She has been promoted several times and is now the Implementation Specialist conducting program evaluation, research and training at the CeaseFire/Cure Violence headquarters in the School of Public health at the University of Illinois at Chicago. She has been featured in numerous newspaper articles, was an invited guest at the 2013 Inaugural Ceremony & Ball in Washington DC. Bianca has also traveled throughout the United States speaking at prisons, universities, and other venues about her life and her work. In addition to her full-time job at CeaseFire, she is writing a book and has begun pursuing her interest in public relations for upcoming music artists part-time. Bianca had just returned from the Grammys when we spoke in February 2015 and shared stories of meeting several music icons on the Staples Center's red carpet, yet she remained humble stating that her immediate plans were to "continue working with CeaseFire to save as many lives as possible."

Education was a major focus for several of the women. As of February 2015, Carleen, Janine, and Julisa had begun work to complete their Bachelor's degrees, while Lynn and Renee were completing their Master's degrees. Like Bianca, the women expressed their commitment to continue their work as peacemakers in their communities, even in the face of pending budget cuts that may affect their jobs:

> I want to always help the sister and brother in the street. I want to start a business that trains those who have records and can't work, but this business will train them to start their own. (Lynn)
>
> I want to focus on school as well as have a successful year decreasing violence through CeaseFire. (Carleen)
>
> One thing is for certain, that I maintain my position in a place where God can continue to use me, so that lives may be saved. I want to be a living testimony of transformation by the renewing of the mind. (Priscilla)

For these women, the time for transformation is now.

NOTES

1. The impetus for this statement comes from the following quote attributed to Albert Einstein, "Without changing our pattern of thought, we will not be able to solve problems we created with our current patterns of thought."
2. See http://www.bjs.gov/content/reentry/recidivism.cfm
3. I hesitate to add a figure depicting the symbol I have described for transformative justice, because of the impossible task envisioning the degrees of each of the three angles. An isosceles triangle may be the best representation, since I believe the foundation provided by the mezzo- and macro-level factors are the fundamental contributors to the transformative justice processes needed a this particular point in time to facilitate the engagement of individuals, yet, I am not comfortable with the assumption that mezzo- and macro-factors are equal contributors to the processes, nor that the processes can or should remain the same over time. The shape of the ideal symbol for transformative justice may be very flat triangle, indicating a time when a majority of individuals have become empowered and actively engaged in transformative processes, or perhaps a circle suggesting that all factors are equitably contributing dynamic and integrated processes of transformative justice.
4. For further information on the impact of State of Illinois budget cuts on CeaseFire, see Thomas A. Corfman's (03/15/2015) article, "Rauner halts funding for CeaseFire" at http://www.chicagobusiness.com/article/20150305/NEWS02/150309960/rauner-halts-funding-for-ceasefire
5. For further information on the State of Illinois budget crisis, see Natasha Korecki's (2/18/2015) article, "10 areas on Rauners chopping block" at http:///www.chicago.suntimes.com/politics/1/71/37879/10-areas-rauners-chopping-block

6. See the TASC Annual Report 2004: Bringing Health & Justice Together, p. 4. Retrieved from http://www2.tasc.org/sites/default/files/Annual%20Report_FINAL.pdf

7. See Angela Davis's quote in "Where do we go from here?" *Essence: Special Collector's Edition,* February 2015, p. 92.

References

Adler, F. (1975). *Sisters in crime.* New York: McGraw Hill.

Ahmed, E., & Braithwaite, V. (2006). Forgiveness, reconciliation, and shame: Three key variables in reducing school bullying. *Journal of Social Issues, 62*(2), 347–370.

Ahmed, E., Harris, N., Braithwaite, J., & Braithwaite, V. (2001). *Shame management through reintegration.* Cambridge: Cambridge University Press.

Alexander, M. (2010). *The new Jim Crow: Mass incarceration in the age of color-blindness.* New York: The New Press.

Agnew, R. (2014). Social Concern and Crime: Moving beyond the Assumption of Simple Self-Interest. *Criminology, 52*(1), 1–32.

Andrews, D. A., & Bonta, J. (2003). *The psychology of criminal conduct* (3rd ed.). Cincinnati, OH: Anderson.

Anderson, E. (2002). *The Code of the Street: Decency, Violence, and the Moral Life of the Inner City*, New York: W.W. Norton.

Anderson, E. (1990). *Streetwise: Race, Class, and Change in an Urban Community*, Chicago: University of Chicago Press.

Austin, J. (2001). Prisoner reentry: Current trends; practices and issues. *Crime and Delinquency. 47*(3), 314–334.

Baca Zinn, M., & Thornton Dill, B. (1996). Theorizing difference from multiracial feminism. *Feminist Studies, 22*(2), 321–331.

Bahr, S. J., Maughan, S. L., Marcos, A. C., & Li, B. (1998). Family, Religiosity, and the Risk of Adolescent Drug Use. *Journal of Marriage and the Family, 60*(4), 979–992.

Baier, C. J., & Wright, B. R. E. (2001). "If you love me, keep my commandments": A meta-analysis of the effect of religion on crime. *Journal of Research in Crime and Delinquency, 38,* 2–21.

Barak, G. (1998). *Integrating Criminologies.* Boston: Allyn & Bacon.

Barrett, J. (2012, September 28). Lend time, treasure and talent to A Safe Haven residents. Retrieved from http://www.examiner.com/article/lend-time-treasure-and-talent-to-a-safe-haven-residents.

Barrett, D. E., Katsiyannis, A., & Zhang, D. (2010). Predictors of Offense Severity, Adjudication, Incarceration, and Repeat Referrals for Juvenile Offenders: A Multicohort Replication Study. *Remedial and Special Education, 31*(4), 261–275.

Bart, P. (1982). How I lost my false consciousness and found women's liberation. *Off Our Backs, 12*(5), 7.

Baruch Bush, R. A., & Folger, J. (1994). *The Promise of Mediation: Responding to Conflict through Empowerment and Recognition.* San Francisco: Jossey-Bass.

Bauman, Z. (2000). *Liquid modernity.* Cambridge, UK: Polity Press.

Becker, H. (1970). Whose side are we on? In Jack D. Douglas (Ed.), *The relevance of Sociology* (pp. 99–111). New York. Appleton-Century-Crofts.

Beale, F. (1995). Double jeopardy: To be Black and female. In B. Guy-Sheftall (Ed.), *Words of fire: An anthology of African-American feminist thought* (pp. 146–155). New York: New Press. (Original work published 1970).

Beck, U. (1992). *Risk Society: Towards a New Modernity.* New Delhi: Sage Publications.

Belknap, J. (2007). *The Invisible Woman: Gender, Crime and Justice.* Belmont, CA: Wadsworth Publishing Company.

Belknap, J., & Holsinger, K. (2006). The Gendered Nature of Risk Factors for Delinquency. *Feminist Criminology. I*(1), 48–71.

Belknap, J., & Shelly, J. K. (1993). The New Lone Ranger: Policewomen on Patrol. *American Journal of Police 12*, 47–75

Belknap, J. (1991). Women in Conflict: An Analysis of Women Correctional Officers. *Women and Criminal Justice, 2*, 89–115.

Benson, M. (2002). *Crime and the Life Course.* Los Angeles, CA: Roxbury.

Berlin, I. (1971). Two Concepts of Liberty. In Isaiah Berlin (Ed.), *Four Essays on Liberty.* (pp. 118–172). New York: Oxford University Press.

Bernard, A. (2014). The intersectional alternative: Explaining female criminality. In DeKeseredy, W. & Dragiewicz, M. (Eds.), *Routledge Major Works: Critical Criminology, Critical Concepts in Criminology Series, Volume VI: Critical Interventions: Engaging Social Justice (*pp. 115–131). London: Routledge.

Bernard, A. (2013). The 21st Century Caribbean woman's question: What is the meaning of freedom? In Cobley, A. & Simpson, V. (Eds.), *Trajectories of Freedom.* Kingston, JA: UWI Press, pp. 192–208.

Bernard, A., & Agozino, O. (2012). Free space & Inner space: A place for reconstructing self and other. *The Journal of Pan African Studies, 5*(6), pp. 56–74.

Black, C. (2014, August 13). The cost of disinvestment in Chicago's West Side. *Chicago Reporter.* Retrieved from http://www.chicagoreporter.com/cost-disinvestment-chicagos-west-side.

Blakemore, K. (2007). *Social Policy: An Introduction.* London: Open University.

Bloom, B., Owen, B., & Covington, S. (2005). Gender-responsive strategies for women offenders: A summary of research, practice, and guiding principles for women offenders. *Gender responsive strategies for women offenders.* Retrieved from http://www.nicic.org/pubs/2005/020418.pdf.

Bloom, B., Owen, B., & Covington, S. (2004). Women offenders and the gendered effects of public policy. *Review of Policy Research, 21*, 31–48.

Bloom, B., Owen, B., & Covington, S. (2003). *Gender-responsive strategies: Research, practice, and guiding principles for women offenders.* Washington, DC: National Institute of Corrections.

Boddie, S., Franklin, R., & Trulear, H. D. (2010). *Healing communities: A framework for congregations in their ministry to families affected by incarceration.* Retrieved from http://ojp.gov/fbnp/pdfs/Healing_Communities.pdf

Bonta, J., Jesseman, R., Ruggge, T., & Cormier, R. (2006). Restorative justice and recidivism: Promises made, promises kept? In Sullivan & L. Tifft (Eds.), *Handbook of restorative justice* (pp. 225–243). Portland, OR: Willan.

Bonta, J., Pang, B., & Wallace-Capretta, S. (1995). Predictors of recidivism among incarcerated female offenders. *The Prison Journal, 75*(3), 277–294.

Bowles, M. A., DeHart, D., & Webb, J. R. (2012). Family Influences on Female Offenders' Substance Use: The Role of Adverse Childhood Events among Incarcerated Women. *Journal of Family Violence, 27*(7), 681–686.

Boyd, E., & Grants, T. (2005). Is gender a factor in perceived prison officer competence? Male prisoners' perceptions in an English dispersal prison. *Criminal Behaviour and Mental Health, 15*(1), 65–74.

Braithwaite, J., & Strang, H. (2001). Introduction: Restorative justice and civil society. In H. Strang & J. Braithwaite (Eds.), *Restorative justice and civil society* (pp. 1–13). Cambridge, UK: Cambridge University Press.

Braithwaite, J. (2002). *Restorative Justice and Responsive Regulation.* New York: Oxford University.

Bratton, W. J. (1999). Great expectations: How higher expectations for police departments can lead to a decrease in crime. In R.H. Langworthy (Ed.), *Measuring what matters: Proceedings from the Police Research Institute meetings* (pp. 11–26). Washington, D.C.: National Institute of Justice.

Britton, D. M. (2004). Feminism in criminology: Engendering the outlaw. In P. J. Schram & B. Koons-Witt (Eds.), *Gendered (in)justice: Theory and practice in feminist criminology* (pp. 49–67). Long Grove, IL: Waveland Press.

Britton, D. (1997). Gendered Organizational Logic: Policy and Practice in Men's and women's Prisons. *Gender and Society, 11*, 796–818.

Broidy, L., & Agnew, R. (1997). Gender and Crime: A General Strain Theory Perspective. *Journal of Research in Crime and Delinquency, 34*(3), 275–306.

Bronfenbrenner, U. (1979). *The Ecology of Human Development: Experiments by Nature and Design.* Cambridge, Massachusetts: Harvard University Press.

Brown, G. (2010). The Intersectionality of Race, Gender, and Reentry: Challenges for African American Women. *American Constitution Society for Law and Policy: Issue Brief,* 1–18.

Brown, K. M. (2002). Review of the book *Public religion and urban transformation: Faith in the City* by Lowell Livezey, *The Journal of Religion, 82*(2), 334–335.

Brown M., & Ross, S. (2010). Mentoring, social capital and desistance: A study of women released from prison. *Australian & New Zealand Journal of Criminology, 43*(1), 31–50.

Browne, A., Miller, B., & Maguin, E. (1999). Prevalence and severity of Lifetime Physical and Sexual Victimization among Incarcerated Women. *International Journal of Law and Psychiatry, 22*(3–4), 301–322.

Burgess-Proctor, A. (2006). Intersections of Race, Class, Gender, and Crime: Future Directions for Feminist Criminology. *Feminist Criminology, 1*(1), 24–47.

Bursik, R. (1988). Social Disorganization and Theories of Crime. *Criminology, 26*(4), 519–551.

Calahan, M. (1986). *Historical corrections statistics in the United States,* 1850–1984. Washington, DC: Bureau of Justice Statistics.

Caputo, G. A. (2009). Early life trauma among women shoplifters and sex workers. *Journal of Child & Adolescent Trauma, 2,* 15–27.

Carlen, P. (1988). *Women, Crime and Poverty.* London: Open University Press.

Carlen, P. (1985). *Criminal Woman.* Cambridge: Polity Press.

Chavis, M. (2001). Testing the assumptions: Who provides social services? In E. J. Dionne, Jr. & M. H. Chen (Eds.), *Sacred places, civic purposes: Should government help faith-based charity?* (pp. 287–296). Washington, DC: Brookings Institution Press.

Cheeseman, K. A., Mullings, J. L., & Marquart, J. W. (2001). Inmate Perceptions of Security Staff across Various Custody Levels. *Corrections Management Quarterly, 5*(2), 41–47.

Cheeseman, K. A., & Worley, R. (2006). Women on the Wing: Inmate Perceptions about Female Correctional Officer Job Competency in a Southern Prison System. *The Southwest Journal of Criminal Justice, 3*(2), 86–106.

Chesney-Lind, M. (1997). *The female offender: Girls, women, and crime.* Thousand Oaks, CA: and London: Sage Publications.

Chesney-Lind, M. (1991). Patriarchy, prisons and jails: A critical look at trends in women's incarceration. *The Prison Journal, 51*(11), 51–67.

Chesney-Lind, M. (1986). Women and crime: The Female Offender. *Signs, 12*(1), 78–96.

Choi, J. J., & Gilbert M. (2010). 'Joe everyday, people off the street': a qualitative study on mediators' roles and skills in victim-offender mediation. *Contemporary Justice Review, 13*(2), 207–227.

City of Chicago Police Department. (2012). *Chicago Murder Analysis Report.* Chicago: City of Chicago Police Department Detective Division.

Clear, T. R., & Karp, D. R. (1999). *The community justice ideal: Preventing crime and achieving justice.* Boulder, CO: Westview.

Clear, T. R., & Suniter, M. T. (2002). Prisoners, prison, and religion: Religion and adjustment to prison. *Journal of Offender Rehabilitation, 35,* 127–159.

Cloward, R., & Ohlin, L. (1960). *Delinquency and Opportunity.* Glencoe, Illinois: Free Press.

Cobbina, J. (2010). Reintegration success and failure: Factors impacting reintegration among incarcerated and formerly incarcerated women. Journal of Offender Rehabilitation. *49*, 210–232

Collins, P. H. (2000). *Black feminist thought: Knowledge, consciousness, and the politics of empowerment* (2nd Ed.). New York: Routledge.

Costello, B. (1997). "On the Logical Adequacy of Cultural Deviance Theories." *Theoretical Criminology, 1*(4), 403–428.

Corcoran, J. (2008). *Groups in social work: A workbook.* Boston: Allyn & Bacon.

Crawford, A., & Newburn, T. (2003). *Youth offending and restorative justice: Implementing reform in youth justice.* Devon, UK: Wilan Publishing.

Crawley, E. (2004). Doing Prison Work: The Public and Private Lives of Prison Officers. Willan Publishing: UK.

Cullen, F. T. (2007). Public Support for Faith-Based Correctional Programs: Should Sacred Places Serve Civic Purposes? *Journal of Offender Rehabilitation, 45*(3/4), 29–46.

Daly, K., & Stephens, D. J. (1995). The "dark figure" of criminology: Towards a Black and multi-ethnic feminist agenda for theory and research. In N. Hahn Rafter & F. Heidensohn (Eds.), *International feminist perspectives in criminology: Engendering a discipline* (pp. 189–215). Philadelphia: Open University Press.

Daly, K., & Chesney-Lind, M. (1988). Feminism and Criminology. *Justice Quarterly, 5*(4): 497–535.

Danzy, J., & Jackson, S. M. (1997). Family preservation and support services: A missed opportunity for kinship care. *Child Welfare, 76*(1), 31–44.

Davis, A. (February 2005). Where do we go from here?" *Essence: Special Collector's Edition*, p. 92.

de Beauvoir, S. (1953). *The Second Sex.* H. M. Parshley (Ed.). New York: Knopf.

DeHart, D. (2008). Pathways to Prison: Impact of victimization in the lives of incarcerated women. *Violence Against Women, 14*(12), 1362–1381.

DeHart, D. (2009). *Polyvictimization among Girls in the Juvenile Justice System: Manifestations an Associations to Delinquency (NCJRS Document #228620).* Columbia: The Center for Child and Family Studies, College of Social Work, University of South Carolina.

DeKeseredy, W., & Perry, B. (2006). *Advancing Critical Criminology: Theory and Application.* Lanham, MD: Lexington Books.

Denzin, N. K. (1989). *Interpretive Interactionism.* Thousand Oaks, CA: Sage Publications.

Denzin, N. K., & Lincoln, Y.S. (2005). *The SAGE handbook of qualitative research.* Thousand Oaks: Sage Publications.

Dilulio, J. J. (2001). Not by faith alone: Religion, crime, and substance abuse. In E. J. Dionne, Jr. & M. H. Chen (Eds.), *Sacred places, civic purposes: Should government help faith-based charity?* (pp. 77–93). Washington, DC: Brookings Institution Press.

DiIulio, J. J. (1995). The coming of the super-predators. *The Weekly Standard,* November *27*, 23–28.

Doll, Y. (2007). Leadership competencies and promotion factors of U.S. women general officers. Published in Tiemann, K. A., Mcneal, R. B., Lucal, B., & Ender, M. G. (Eds.), *The intersections collection: Pearson custom sociology* (pp. 73–96). Boston, MA: Pearson Custom Publishing.

Dumke, M. (2013, March 1). School closings: The latest blow to neighborhoods already reeling from disinvestment. *Chicago Reader.* Retrieved from http://www.chicagoreader.com/Bleader/archives/2013/03/01/school-closings-the-latest-blow-to-neighborhoods-already-reeling-from-disinvestment.

Dyck, D. (2000). Reaching toward a structurally responsive training and practice of restorative justice. *Contemporary Justice Review, 3*(3), 239.

Eitle, D., & Turner, R. J. (2002). Exposure to Community Violence and Young Adult Crime: The Effects of Witnessing Violence, Traumatic Victimization, and Other Stressful Life Events. *Journal of Research in Crime and Delinquency, 39*(2), 214–237.

Fagan, A. (2001). The Gender Cycle of Violence: Comparing the Effects of Child Abuse and Neglect on Criminal Offending for Males and Females. *Violence and Victims, 14*(4), 457–474.

Fanon, F. (1963). *The Wretched of the Earth*. Middlesex: Penguin.

Farrall, S. (2002). *Rethinking what works with offenders: Probation, social context and desistance from crime.* Devon, UK and Portland, Oregon: Willan Publishing.

Farrall, S. (2004). Social capital and offender reintegration: Making probation desistance focused. In Maruna, S. & Immarigeon (Eds.), *After crime and punishment: Pathways to offender reintegration* (pp. 57–84). Devon, UK and Portland, Oregon: Willan Publishing.

Fisher, M. L., & Exline, J. J. (2006). Self-forgiveness versus excusing: The roles of remorse, effort and acceptance of responsibility. *Self and Identity, 5*(2), 127–146.

Foster, M. (1993). Othermothers: Exploring the educational philosophy of Black American women teachers. In M. Arnot & K. Weiler (Eds.), *Feminism and social justice in education: International perspectives* (pp. 101–123). Washington, DC: Falmer Press.

Fuller, J. R. (1998). *Criminal justice: A peacemaking perspective.* Boston: Allyn and Bacon.

Fuller, J. (2003). Peacemaking Criminology, in Schwartz, M. D and Hatty, S. E. (Eds.), *Controversial issues in critical criminology* (pp. 85–99). Cincinnati, OH: Anderson Publishing.

Garmezy, N. (1993). Risk and resilience. In D.C. Funder, R.D. Parke, C. Tomlinson-Keasey & K. Widaman (Eds.), *Studying lives through time: Personality and development* (pp. 377–398). Washington, DC: American Psychological Association.

Gau, J. M., & Brunson, R. K. (2010). Procedural justice and order maintenance policing: A study of inner-city young men's perceptions of police legitimacy. *Justice Quarterly, 27*(2), 255–279.

Gaum, G., Hoffman, S., & Venter, J. H. (2006). Factors that influence adult recidivism: An exploratory study in Pollsmoor prison. *South African Journal of Psychology, 36*(2), 407–424.

Geertz, C. (1973). Thick description: Toward an interpretative theory of culture. In *The interpretation of cultures: Selected essays* (pp. 3–30). New York: Basic Books.

Gelsthorpe, L., & Morris, A. (2000). Something old, something borrowed, something blue, but something new? A comment on the prospectus for restorative justice under the Crime and Disorder Act 1998. *Criminal Law Review,* January, 18–30.

Gibson, P. A. (2005). Intergenerational parenting from the perspective of African American grandmothers. *Family Relations, 54,* 280–297.

Glaze, L., & Maruschak, L. (2008). *Parents in prison and their minor children.* Washington, D.C.: Bureau of Justice Statistics.

Giddens, A. (1991). *Modernity and self identity: Self and society in the late modern age.* Stanford, CA: Stanford University Press.

Gilfus, M. (1992). From Victims to Survivors to Offenders: Women's Routs of Entry and Immersion into Street Crime. *Women and Criminal Justice, 4*(1), 63–89.

Gilligan, C. (1988). *In a different voice: Psychological theory and women's development.* Cambridge, Mass.: Harvard University Press.

Gilligan, C. (1982). Adolescent development reconsidered. In C. Gilligan, J.V. Ward and J. McLean Taylor (Eds.), *Mapping the moral domain.* Cambridge, Mass.: Harvard University Press.

Gordon, V. V. (1987). *Black women, feminism and Black liberation: Which way?* Chicago: Third World Press.

Greer, K. (2008). *When women hold the keys: Gender, leadership, and correctional policy.* Centerville, UT: MTC Institute.

Guerino, P., Harrison, P.M., & Sabol, W. (2011). *Prisoners in 2010.* Washington, DC: Bureau of Justice Statistics.

Hahn Rafter, N., & Stanko, E. A. (1982). *Judge, lawyer, victim thief: women, gender roles and criminal justice.* Boston: Northeastern University Press.

Hall, J. H., & Fincham, F. D. (2005). Self-forgiveness: The stepchild of forgiveness research. *Journal of Social and Clinical Psychology, 24*(5), 621–637.

Hancy, C. (2002). *The psychological impact of incarceration: Implications for post-prison adjustment.* Washington, DC: Urban Institute Press.

Harcourt, B., & Ludwig, J. (2006). "Broken Windows: New Evidence from New Evidence from New York City and a Five City Social Experiment." *The University of Chicago Law Review, 73*(1), 271–320.

Harding, S. (Ed.). (2004). T*he Feminist Standpoint Theory Reader.* New York and London: Routledge.

Harm, N., & Phillips S. (2001). You can't go home again: Women and criminal recidivism. *Journal of Offender Rehabilitation, 32*(3), 3–21.

Harris, M. K. (2004). An expansive, transformative view of restorative justice. *Contemporary Justice Review, 7*(1), 117–141.

Harris, P. M., & Keller, K. S. (2005). Ex-offenders need not apply: The criminal background check in hiring decisions. *Journal of Contemporary Criminal Justice, 21,* 6–30.

Howell, J. C. (2009). *Preventing and reducing juvenile delinquency: A comprehensive framework* (2nd Ed.*).* Thousand Oaks, CA: Sage Publications, Inc.

Hirt, J. B., Amelink, C. T., McFeeters, B. B., & Srayhorn, T. L. (2008). A system of othermothering: Student affairs administrator' perceptions of relationships with students at historically Black colleges. *Journal of Student Affairs Research & Practice, 45*(2), 210–236.

Hochschild, A. (1979). Emotion work, feeling rules, and social structure. *American Journal of Sociology, 85,* 551–575.

Holmgren, M. R. (1998). Self-forgiveness and responsible moral agency. *The Journal of Value Inquiry, 32,* 75–91.

hooks, b. (1984). *Feminist Theory: From margin to center.* Boston: South End Press.

Holtfreter, K. L., & Morash, M. (2003). The needs of women offenders: Implications for correctional programming. *Women and Criminal Justice, 14*, 137–160.

Jackson, D. (2013, September 28). Chicago development programs bypass Austin. *Chicago Tribune.* Retrieved from http://articles.chicagotribune.com/2013-09-28/news/ct-met-austin-development-history-20130929_1_south-austin-16-neighborhoods-economic-development

Jackson, F. L. (2001). Freedom and the tie that binds: Marriage as an ethical institution. *Animus, 6*, 115–144.

Jacobson, M. (2005). *Downsizing prisons: How to reduce crime and end mass incarceration.* New York: New York University.

James, D., & Glaze, L. (2006). *Mental health problems of prison and jail inmates.* Washington, DC: Bureau of Justice Statistics.

Jang, S. J., & Johnson, B. R. (2001). Neighborhood disorder, individual religiosity, and adolescent use of illicit drugs: A test of multilevel hypothesis. *Criminology, 39*(1), 109–144.

Johnson, B. R. (2004). Religious programs and recidivism among former inmates in Prison Fellowship programs: A long-term follow-up study. *Justice Quarterly, 21*, 329–354.

Johnson, B. R., Jang, S. J., De Li, S., & Larson, D. B. (2000). The "invisible institution" and black youth crime: The church as an agency of local social control. *Journal of Youth and Adolescence, 29*, 479–498.

Johnson, B. R., Larson, D. B., De Li, S., & Jang, S. J., (2000). Escaping from the crime of inner cities: Church attendance and religious salience among disadvantaged youth. *Justice Quarterly, 17*, 377–391.

Johnson, B. R., Jang, S. J., Larson, D. B., & De Li, S. (2001). Does adolescent religious commitment matter? A reexamination of the effects of religiosity on delinquency. *Journal of Research in Crime and Delinquency, 38*(1), 22–44.

Johnson, B. R., Larson, D. B., & Pitts, T. (1997). Religious programs, institutional adjustment, and recidivism among former inmates in Prison Fellowship programs. *Justice Quarterly, 14*, 145–166.

Johnstone, G. (2002). *Restorative Justice: Ideas, Values, Debates.* Cullompton: Willan Publishing.

Jorgensen, D. L. (1989). Participant Observation: A Methodology for Human Studies. Newbury Park, CA: Sage Publications.

Kaplow, J. B., Curran, P. J., Dodge, K. A. (2002). Child, Parent and Peer Predictors of Early-Onset Substance Use: A Multisite Longitudinal Study. *Journal of Abnormal Child Psychology, 30*(3), 199–216.

Kelling, G. L. (2000). Why did people stop committing crimes? An essay about criminology and ideology. *Fordham Urban Law Journal, 28*, 567–586.

Kelling, G. L., & Bratton. (1998). Declining crime rates: Insiders' view of the New York City story. *Journal of Criminal Law and Criminology, 88*(4), 1217–1231.

Kelly, M. (1994). *Critique and power: recasting the Foucault/Habermas debate.* Boston: MIT Press.

Kerpelman, J. L., & Smith-Adcock, S. (2005). Female Adolescents' Delinquent Activity: The Intersection of Bonds to Parents and Reputation Enhancement. *Youth & Society, 37*(2), 176–200.

Kiesner, J., Poulin, F., & Dishion, T. J. (2010). Adolescent Substance Use with Friends: Moderating and Mediating Effects of Parental Monitoring and Peer Activity Contexts. *Merrill-Palmer Quarterly, 56*(4), 529–556.

King, D. K. (1988). Multiple jeopardy, multiple consciousness: The context of Black feminist ideology. *Signs: Journal of Women in Culture and Society, 14*(1), 42–72.

Kretzmann, J. P., & McKnight. J. (1996). *A Guide to Mapping and Mobilizing the Economic Capacities of Local Residents: A Community Building Workbook from the Assets-Based Community Development Institute.* Evanston, Illinois: Center for Urban Affairs and Policy Research, Neighborhood Innovations Network.

Lambert, E. G., Paoline, E. A., Hogan, N. L., & Baker, D. N. (2007). Gender Similarities and Differences in Correctional Staff Work Attitudes and Perceptions of the Work Environment. *Western Criminology Review, 8(1),* 16–31.

Laub, J. H., & Sampson, R. (2003). *Shared beginnings, divergent lives: Delinquent boys to age 70.* Cambridge, MA: Harvard University Press.

La Vigne, N., Visher, C., & Castro, J. (2004). *Chicago Prisoners' Experiences Returning Home.* Washington, DC: Urban Institute.

Lipsky, M. (2010). *Street level bureaucracy: Dilemmas of the individual in public services.* New York: The Russell Sage Foundation.

Locke, J. (1988). *Two Treatises of Government.* Laslett, Peter (Ed.). Cambridge: Cambridge University Press.

Lonsway, K., Moore, M., Harrington, C. P., Smeal, E., & Spillar, K. (2003). Hiring and retaining more women: The advantages to law enforcement agencies. *National Center for Women and Policing, a Division of the Feminist Majority Foundation.* URL: http://www.womenandpolicing.org/pdf/NewAdvantagesReport.pdf

Lombroso, C. (1958). *The female offender.* New York: Philosophical Library.

Lombroso, C., & Guglielmo, F. (2004). *Criminal woman, the prostitute, and the normal woman* (N. Han Rafter & M. Gibson, Eds.). Durham, NC: Duke University Press.

Lorde, A. (1984). *Sister Outsider.* Berkeley, CA: Crossing Press.

Lucken, K., & Ponte, L. (2008). Ajust measure of forgiveness: Reforming occupational licensing regulations for ex-inmates using BFOQ analysis. *Law & Policy, 30*(1), 46–72.

Lynch, M. J. (1996). Class, race, gender and criminology: Structured choices and the life course. In D. Milovanovic & M. D. Schwartz (Eds.), *Race, gender, and class in criminology: The intersections* (pp. 3–28). New York: Garland.

Maidment, M. R. (2006a). *Doing time on the outside: Deconstructing the benevolent community.* Toronto: University of Toronto Press.

Maidment, M. (2006b). Transgressing Boundaries: Feminist Perspectives in Criminology. In W. DeKeseredy & B. Perry (Eds.), *Advancing Critical Criminology: Theory and Application* (pp. 43–62). Lanham, Maryland: Lexington Books.

Malik-Kane, K., & Visher, C. (2008). *Health and prisoner reentry: How physical, mental, and substance abuse conditions shape the process of reintegration.* Washington, DC: Urban Institute.

Marshall, T. F. (1999). *Restorative Justice: An Overview.* London: Home Office Research Development and Statistics Directorate.

Martin, A. (26 February 2015). The chronically homeless. *The New York Times.* Retrieved from http://mobile.nytimes.com/2015/02/26/opinion/the-chroniclly-homeless.html?referrer=

Maruna, S. (2001). *Making good: How ex-convicts reform and rebuild their lives.* Washington, DC: American Psychological Association.

Maruschak, L. (2008). *Medical problems of prisoners.* Washington, D.C.: Bureau of Justice Statistics.

Matsueda, R. (1997). "Cultural Deviance Theory": The Remarkable Persistence of a Flawed Term. *Theoretical Criminology, 1*(4), 429–452.

Maxwell, G., & Morris, A. (2002). The role of shame, guilt, and remorse in restorative justice processes for young people. In E. G. M. Weitekamp & H. Kerner (Eds.), *Restorative justice: Theoretical foundations* (pp. 267–284). Portland, OR: Willan Publishing.

McKnight, J. (1995). The Careless Society: Community and Its Counterfeits. New York: Basic Books.

McMillen, J. C., Morris, L., & Sherraden, M. (2004). Ending social work's grudge match: Problems versus strengths. *Families in Society, 85*(3), 317–325.

McRoberts, O. (2002). *Religion, reform, community: Examining the idea of church-based prisoner reentry.* Retrieved from http://www.urban.org/uploaded-pdf/410802_religion.pdf

Merton, R. (1968). Social theory and social structure, enlarged edition. New York, NY: Free Press.

Messerschmidt, J. (1993). *Masculinities and Crime: Critique and Reconceptualization of Theory.* Lantham, MD: Rowman and Littlefield.

Moffitt, T., & Caspi, A. (2001). Childhood predictors of differentiate life-course persistent offenders and adolescent limited antisocial pathways among males and females. *Development and Psychopathy, 13*, 355–375.

Morris, A. (1987). *Women, Crime and Criminal Justice.* Oxford, England: Basil Blackwell.

Morris, A. D. (1986). *The Origins of the Civil Rights Movement: Black Communities Organizing for Change.* New York: Free Press.

Morris, R. (2000). *Stories of transformative justice.* Toronto: Canadian Scholars Press.

Morris, R. (1995). *Penal Abolition: The Practical Choice.* Toronto: Canadian Scholar's Press.

Morton, J. B. (Ed.). (1991) Change, Challenge & Choices: Women's Role in Modern Corrections. Waldorf, MD: St. Mary's Press.

Morton, J. B. (1981). Women in Correctional Employment: Where are they now and where are they headed. In B.H. Olsen (Ed.), *Women in Corrections* (pp. 7–16). Lanhman, MD: American Correctional Association.

Muraskin, R. (2012). *Women and Justice: It's a Crime. Fifth Edition.* New Jersey: Prentice Hall.

National Association of State Budget Officers (1985–2012). *State Expenditure Report Series.* Washington, DC: National Association of State Budget Officers.

Nellis, A. (2013). *Life Goes On: The Historic Rise in Life Sentences in America.* Washington, DC: The Sentencing Project.

Nouwen, H. (1972). *The wounded healer.* New York: Doubleday.

O'Brien, P. (2001). *Making it in the ''free world:'' Women in transition from prison.* New York, NY: State University of New York Press.

O'Connor, T. P., & Perreyclear, M. (2002). Prison religion in action and its influence on offender rehabilitation. *Journal of Offender Rehabilitation, 35,* 11–33.

Oakley, A. (1981). Interviewing women: a contradiction in terms. In Helen Roberts (Ed.), *Doing Feminist Research* (pp. 30–62). London: Routledge & Kegan Paul.

Oselin, S. (2014). *Leaving Prostitution: Getting Out and Staying Out of Sex Work.* New York: NYU Press.

Owen, B. (1998). *"In the Mix": Struggle and Survival in a Women's Prison.* Albany, NY: SUNY Press.

Patterson, G. R. (1979). A performance theory for coercive family interactions. In R. Cairns (Ed.), *Social interaction: Methods, analysis, and illustration* (pp. 119–162). Hillsdale, NJ: Lawrence Erlbaum Associates.

Pepinsky, H. F. (2013). Peacemaking Criminology. *Critical Criminology, 21*(3), 319–339.

Pepinsky, H., Quinney, R. (Eds.). (1991). *Criminology as peacemaking.* Bloomington: Indiana University Press.

Pogorzelski, W., Wolff, N., Pan, K., & Blitz, C. (2005). Behavioral Health Problems, Ex-Offender Reentry Policies, and the "Second Chance Act." *American Journal of Public Health. 95*(10), 1718–1724.

Potter, H. (2006). An Argument for Black Feminist Criminology: Understanding African American Women's Experiences with Intimate Partner Abuse Using an Integrated Approach. *Feminist Criminology, 1*(2), 106–124.

Price, M. (2000). Place, Race, and History: The Social Mission of Downtown Churches in Lowell Livezey (Ed.), *Public Religion and Urban Transformation.* (pp. 57–82). New York: New York University Press.

Prochaska, J., & DiClemente, C. (1983). Stages and processes of self-change in smoking: toward an integrative model of change. *Journal of Consulting and Clinical Psychology, 5,* 390–395.

Prochaska, J., & DiClemente, C. (1997). The transtheoretical model of health and behavior change. *American Journal of Health Promotion, 12,* 38–48.

Putnam, R. D. (2001). *Bowling Alone: The Collapse and Revival of American Community.* New York: Simon & Schuster.

Quinney, R. (2000). The way of peace: On crime, suffering and service. In *Bearing witness to crime and social justice* (pp. 179–192). Albany, NY: State University of New York Press.

Rapp, C. A. (1997). *The strengths model: Case management with people suffering from severe and persistent mental illness.* New York: Oxford Univ. Press.

Reger, J. (2004). Organizational "emotion work" through consciousness-raising: An analysis of a feminist organization. *Qualitative Sociology, 27*(2), 205–219.

Reiman, J. (2003). The *Rich Get Richer and the Poor Get Prison: Ideology, Class, and Criminal Justice,* Seventh Edition. Boston: Allyn & Bacon.

Richie, B. E. (2004). Feminist Ethnographies of Women in Prison. *Feminist Studies, 30*(2), 438–450.

Richie, B. E. (2001). Challenges incarcerated women face as they return to their communities: Findings from life history interviews. *Crime and Delinquency, 47,* 368–389.

Richie, B. E. (1996). *Compelled to crime: The gender entrapment of battered Black women.* New York: Routledge.

Riek, B. (2010). Transgressions, guilt, and forgiveness: a model of seeking forgiveness. *Journal of Psychology and Theology, 38*(4), 246–254.

Rousseau, J. (1946). A Discourse on the Origin of Inequality. In G. D. H. Cole (Ed.), *The Social Contract and Discourses.* New York: E. P. Dutton.

Saleebey, D. (2005). *The strengths perspective in social work practice.* 4th Ed. Boston: Allyn & Bacon.

Sampson, R. J., & Wikstrom, P. (2006). How does Community Context Matter? Social Mechanism and the Explanation of Crime. In *The Explanation of Crime: Context, Mechanisms, and Development,* 31–60. New York and Cambridge: Cambridge University Press.

Sampson, R., & Laub, J. H. (1993). *Crime in the making: Pathways and turning points through life.* Cambridge, MA: Harvard University Press.

Salisbury, E. J., & Van Voorhis, P. (2009). Gendered Pathways: A Quantitative Investigation of Women Probationers' Paths to Incarceration. *Criminal Justice and Behavior, 36*(6): 541–566.

Shaw, C., & McKay, H. (1969). *Juvenile Delinquency and Urban Areas.* Chicago: The University of Chicago Press.

Skogan, W., Hartnett, S., Bump, N., & Dubois, J. (2009). *Evaluation of CeaseFire-Chicago.* Washington, DC: National Institute of Justice, Office of Justice Programs. Retrieved from https://www.ncjrs.gov/pdffiles1/nij/grants/227181.pdf.

Sheafor, B., &. Horejsi, C. (2003). *Techniques and guidelines for social work practice.* 6th Ed. Boston: Pearson Education, Inc.

Solis, C., Portillos, E. L., & Brunson, R. K. (2009). Latino youths' experiences with and perceptions of involuntary police encounters. *Annals of the American Academy of Political and Social Science, 623,* 39–51.

Soskis, B. (2001). What religion cannot do: Act of Faith. *The New Republic. 229*(9), 20–23.

Sudbury, J. (2003). Toward a Holistic Anti-Violence Agenda: Women of Color as Radical Bridge-Builders. *Social Justice, 30*(3), 134–139.

Sullivan, D., & Tifft, L. (2010). *Restorative justice: Healing the foundations of our everyday lives.* 2nd Ed. Boulder, CO: Lynne Rienner

Sullivan, D., & Tifft, L. (2000). *Restorative justice as a transformative process: The application of restorative justice principles to our everyday lives.* Voorheesville, NY: Mutual Aid Press.

Sutherland, E. H. (1939). *Principles of Criminology*. Philadelphia, PA: Lippincott.

Thompson, M., & Cummings, D. (2010). Enhancing the career development of individuals who have criminal records. *Career Development Quarterly, 58*, 209–218.

Tong, R. (1989). *Feminist Thought: A comprehensive introduction*. London: Routledge.

Tonry, M. (2014). Remodeling American Sentencing: A Ten-Step Blueprint for Moving Past Mass Incarceration. *Criminology and Public Policy, 13*(4), 503–534.

Tonry, M. (1995). *Malign Neglect: Race, Crime, and Punishment in America*. New York: Oxford University Press.

Travis, J. (2005). *But they all come back: Facing the challenges of prisoner reentry*. Washington, DC: The Urban Institute Press.

Trottera, C., McIvorb, G., & Sheehana, R. (2012). The Effectiveness of Support and Rehabilitation Services for Women Offenders. *Australian Social Work. 65*(1), 6–20.

Turner, R. J., & Lloyd, D. A. (1999). The Stress Process and the Social Distribution of Depression. *Journal of Health and Social Behavior, 40*(4), 374–404.

Tutu, D. (1999). *No future without forgiveness*. New York: Doubleday.

Umbreit, M. (1995). Restorative justice through mediation: The impact of offenders facing their victims in Oakland. *Journal of Law and Social Work, 5*, 1–13.

VanDenBerg, J., & Grealish, E. (1996). Individualized Services and Supports through the Wraparound Process: Philosophy and Procedures. *Journal of Child and Family Studies*, *5*(1), 7–21.

Vanderbilt-Adriance, E., & Shaw, D. S. (2008). Protective factors and the development of resilience in the context of neighborhood disadvantage. *Journal of Abnormal Child Psychology, 36*(6), 887–901.

Visher, C., Yahner, J., & La Vigne. N. (2010). *Life after Prison: Tracking the Experiences of Male Prisoners Returning to Chicago, Cleveland, and Houston*. Washington, DC: Urban Institute.

Visher, C., Kachnowski, V., La Vigne, N., & Travis, J. (2004). *Baltimore Prisoners' Experiences Returning Home*. Washington, DC: Urban Institute.

Visher, C. (2005). *Chicago communities and prisoner reentry*. Retrieved from http://www.urban.org/UploadedPDF/311225_chicago_communities.pdf

Vold, G. B. (1958). *Theoretical Criminology*. New York: Oxford University Press.

Walmsley, R. (2013). *World Population List,* 10th Ed. Essex: International Centre for Prison Studies.

Weaver, E. (2013). Desistance, reflexivity and relationality: A case study. *European Journal of Probation, 5,* 71–88.

Weitzer, R., & Brunson, R. K. (2009). Strategic responses to the police among inner-city youth. *Sociological Quarterly, 50,* 235–256.

Wilson, J. Q. (1995). Crime and Public Policy. In J. Q. Wilson & J. Petersilia (Eds.), *Crime and Public Policies for Crime Control* (pp. 619–630). San Francisco: Institute for Contemporary Studies.

Wilson, J. Q., & Kelling, G. L. (1982). Broken Windows: The Police and Neighborhood Safety. *Atlantic Monthly, 249*(3), 29–38.

Wing, A. K. (Ed.). (2003). *Critical race feminism: A reader* (2nd Ed.). New York: New York University Press.

Women's Prison Association. (2009). *Mothers, infants and imprisonment: A national look at prison nurseries and community-based alternatives.* New York, NY: Women's Prison Association, Institute on Women & Criminal Justice. Retrieved from http://www.wpaonline.org/pdf/Mothers%20Infants%20and%20Imprisonment%20 2009.pdf

Woodyatt, L., & Wenzel, M. (2013). Self-forgiveness and restoration of an offender following an interpersonal transgression. *Journal of Social and Clinical Psycology, 32*(2), 225–259.

Wuthnow, R. (2004), *Saving America: Faith-based services and the future of civil society.* Princeton, NJ: Princeton University Press.

Young, J. (1997). Left realist criminology: radical in its analysis, realist in its policy. In M. Maguire (Ed.), *The Oxford Handbook of Criminology,* 2nd Ed., Oxford: Oxford University Press.

Zehr, H. (2005; 2002). *The Little Book of Restorative Justice.* Intercourse, PA: Good Books.

Zehr, H. (1990). *Changing Lenses: A New Focus on Crime and Justice.* Scottsdale, PA: Herald Press.

Zimmer, B. (2005). The effect of faith-based programs in reducing recidivism and substance abuse of ex-offenders. *Journal of Community Corrections, 14,* 7–19.

Zimring, F., Hawkins, G., & Kamin, S. (2001). *Punishment and Democracy: Three Strikes and You're Out in California.* New York: Oxford University Press.

Zahn, M., Agnew, R., Fishbein, D., Miller, S., Winn, D., Dakoff, G., & Chesney-Lind, M. (2010). *Girls Study Group: Understanding and Responding to Girls' Delinquency.* Washington, DC: United States Department of Justice.

Index

About the Author

April Bernard received her doctorate in Human Development and Social Policy at Northwestern University's School of Education and Social Policy. Prior to joining Chicago State University in 2012, she worked as a consultant with the United Nations Development Program Caribbean Human Development Report on Crime and Citizen Security and served as a deputy dean of the Faculty of Social Sciences at the University of the West Indies in Barbados where she also lectured in Sociology. Her articles have appeared in *Feminist Criminology,* the *Journal of the Institute of Justice & International Studies*, and *The Journal of Pan African Studies* among others. Her work was also featured in the *Routledge Major Works: Critical Criminology, Critical Concepts in Criminology Series, Volume IV: Critical Interventions: Engaging Social Justice* (2014).

3.5